One of Us

England's Greatest Rugby Players

Phil McGowan
With a foreword by Stuart Lancaster

AMBERLEY

Acknowledgements

Thanks to Mai, Jake and Alice McGowan, Stuart Lancaster, Dave Barton, Jane Baron and all the staff and volunteers at the World Rugby Museum and Amberley Publish[ing].

First published 2015

Amberley Publishing
The Hill, Stroud
Gloucestershire, GL5 4EP

www.amberley-books.com

British Library Cataloguing in Publication Data.
A catalogue record for this book is available from the British Library.

ISBN 978 1 4456 5102 6 (print)
ISBN 978 1 4456 5103 3 (ebook)

Typesetting and Origination by Amberley Publishing.
Printed in the UK.

Contents

Foreword

Pulling on a rugby jersey means a great deal.

The shirt represents the character, culture and tradition of a club and supplies a link of continuity that binds those who wear them to all those who have worn them in the past.

To be selected to play for England at any level means that you are one of the most gifted players of your generation.

Selection to the full side enters you into an elite group of players numbering less than 1,400 since 1871. It also means that you are a part of the oldest tradition in international rugby.

Players always talk about the honour of pulling on an England rugby jersey, and it is an honour. But it should not be seen as the end of a journey. It is the start. Every player to have inherited that jersey at any time has had a responsibility to continue that tradition of success.

The names of all of those to have represented England are written on the interior wall of the England dressing room. Ten of those for each position are listed behind the space where each member of the current squad prepares on a match-day under the heading 'One of Us'.

No player gets to keep his England shirt forever but it is the example set by these 150 players and their achievements to which the current generation must aspire.

Phil made this selection. Mine or yours might differ but the players whose lives and careers are recorded in this book give some indication of type of character required to succeed as an England rugby player.

Stuart Lancaster

Introduction

In January 2015 the total number of players to have represented the senior men's England side stood at 1,367. Contained within this number is the whole sweeping narrative of English international rugby, begun in 1871 when two teams of gentleman turned out at Raeburn Place in Edinburgh.

Their story begins in the Victorian age when those that governed the sport were also those who played it. Of the original English Twenty, ten were former pupils of Rugby School, young men trained in leadership as captains of industry and administrators of the British Empire. Thirteen would play only once for their country but others proved to be more indispensable. Distinguished among them was Fred Stokes, England's first captain.

In these early days the game evolved rapidly and innovators such as prototype half-back Alan Rotherham were able to fundamentally alter our understanding of how the game should be played, paving the way for the successes of the Gurdon brothers, as the Home Nations Championship became a four-horse race for the first time.

After the game had taken root it then began to grow. In the urban industrial centres of the north, locals were intrigued to see sportsmen wearing the colours of their town. Never short on civic pride, local contests became spectacles which led in turn to further participation. In the late 1880s, with Yorkshire to the fore, an influx of new working-class players fundamentally altered the make-up of the national side. Little Dicky Lockwood, known in West Yorkshire as the 'world's wonder' was joined by the likes of Pusher Yiend and Jack Toothill as England took on and defeated all-comers in 1892.

But this fleeting moment of unity and excellence was to be short-lived. Divisions over the issue of broken time payments drove a wedge through the heart of the English game resulting in the Great Schism of 1895. Lockwood and Co. were lost to the rival code for a century and, bereft of her star performers, the English team sputtered and stalled.

Despite all this England rugby remained a ready source of inspiration. Battling personal adversity and racial discrimination, Jimmy Peters blazed a trail for black sportsmen the world over by making his debut in 1906. Before him the magnificent resistance of the likes of several-limbed Octopus Gamlin provided rare beacons in the fog of adversity.

As of 1910 England would play her home games at a place that has since become synonymous with the sport. 'If a country is going to have a national rugby ground it may as well be the best in the world. Which Twickenham is' wrote Wallace Reyburn in 1975.

Fly-half Adrian Stoop set about assembling a team that could match the standards of their new home. This he did with the likes of Cherry Pillman and Bruno Brown instigating the first golden era of English rugby, culminating in Norman Wodehouse's Grand Slam of 1913 and Ronnie Poulton's a year later.

Flanders Fields then set about claiming the bravest men from around the world as the First World War offered a truer test of men's courage. English rugby rose admirably to the challenge but many were lost, including her Grand Slam winning captain of 1914.

When peace came some old faces such as Dave Davies and Cyril Lowe returned and helped usher in another golden period during which the likes of William Wavell Wakefield, Tommy Voyce and Ronald Cove-Smith would deliver unprecedented success on the field.

The 1930s was a period of retrenchment for attacking rugby as lithe runners were replaced by stouter men such as Bernard Gadney and Tuppy Owen-Smith. Still, there was room for moments of brilliance provided by the likes of Hal Sever and a certain Russian Prince who lit up the field in 1936.

Obolensky would not see out the Second World War, and it was with diminished reserves that Nim Hall reassembled his teams in 1947.

The flair of Jeff Butterfield and Peter Jackson allowed England to rise again but it would take a dose of Lancastrian grit in the shape of Eric Evans before they once again stood on the shoulders of their rivals. Into the midfield came Dickie Jeeps and Richard Sharp as the nation began to swing to the sound of the 1960s.

Save for John Pullin's heroics in the southern hemisphere, England spent most of the 1970s looking with envy at the success of their opponents. Still through these lean years they blooded enough warriors – Fran Cotton, Peter Wheeler, Bill Beaumont and Tony Neary – so that by the end of the decade they had a pack of gnarled veterans to fall back on. Younger men such as Mike Slemen and Clive Woodward came into the backs and England returned to the top for the first time in a long time in 1980.

As that decade wore on Rory Underwood, Wade Dooley and Rob Andrew found their way into the team. Then came Brian Moore, Jason Leonard, Will Carling, Jeremy Guscott and others and all of a sudden England stood head and shoulders above their northern rivals. A period of domination unseen since the 1920s followed and England came within a whisker of conquering them all at a home World Cup in 1991.

Then, without pause for breath, the side was bolstered by the first faces from the next great side as Martin Johnson and Lawrence Dallaglio ensured that English success would continue deep into the 1990s. Leonard remained as Neil Back, Richard Hill, Matt Dawson and Jonny Wilkinson came through and began to shape the greatest team that England has so far known. The icing on the cake was a rugby league convert called Jason Robinson, and England began to sweep all aside.

2003 was the year that England won everything. No side before or since has claimed a 6-Nations Grand Slam and Rugby World Cup in the same calendar year.

Inevitably those lofty heights could not be maintained indefinitely, but the story goes on and further great players have since taken the field. Andrew Sheridan, Steve Thompson, Phil Vickery, and Nick Easter would lead England to a second consecutive World Cup Final in 2007.

At Raeburn Place in 1871, twenty players took to the field, many occupying positions that bore different names and served different functions to that which we would recognise today. Thus the task of comparing so many great players from so many different eras is an impossible one.

Physically, players have adapted to suit the rules. Initially training of any kind was considered bad form for amateurs but, since 1995, professional attitudes have placed a premium on winning. Changing diets and a better understanding of sports science have allowed rugby players to achieve a muscle mass that would have been unobtainable in previous eras.

All of these factors mean that any speculative attempts to devise lists are a matter of conjecture. Yet every player, on receipt of a white jersey, has a window of opportunity in which to make his or her mark. These lists were compiled to highlight some of those who did. There are of course more.

I hope you will enjoy reading and that this book will further reinforce why the red rose of England remains a badge of honour and a symbol of pride for all those who wear it.

Phil McGowan

Inside the England Dressing Room

The Rowland Hill Memorial Gates, unveiled in 1929, were originally located outside the south-west corner of the stadium, over a dusty path that had had once been used as a famer's access route before the stadium was even built. When the West Stand was rebuilt in 1995 they were moved to their present location, parallel with the West Stand on the other side of the concourse to the 'Spirit of Rugby' where both teams enter the stadium on match-day.

For this reason every England team to have played at Twickenham since 1995 has passed through the gates on arrival at the stadium. Because of their age they are too narrow for coaches to enter and so players pass through on foot.

In 2013 Stuart Lancaster encouraged his coach driver to park towards the rear of the West Car Park, beginning the ritual of the England captain leading his side through a tunnel of supporters on his way to the home entrance to the West Stand. In this way the players are able to soak up the carnival atmosphere of match-day and feel for themselves the volume of support from the many cheering England fans who have gathered to acknowledge their team.

The captain then leads his side across the west concourse and through a side door to the left of the Spirit of Rugby. On their right they pass a mural that details the history and development of the game from its humble

England players entering the stadium.

beginnings at Rugby School to the present, the other side of which are two bronze plaques that bear the names of forty-one of their predecessors who gave their lives in the First and Second World Wars.

Player's tunnel

Wall of Achievement.

Now the players stand at the far end of the player's tunnel that bears the flag of St George made up of dozens of images and messages of support from England fans all over the world. They turn sharp left and into the England dressing room.

Before entering they pass a darkened wall of achievement. On this are records of England's greatest victories, record cap holders, try and point scorers and trophies. The intention here is not to intimidate the players but simply to remind them that by entering this space they are entering into a tradition that stretches back to 1871, a tradition of success, and one that they, as representatives of England, have a responsibility to maintain.

Inside the dressing room a circular motif on the ceiling records the core values – teamwork, respect, enjoyment, discipline and sportsmanship. On the left a roll of honour records the names of every player to have been capped by England since the very first game in 1871.

Behind each of the players' seats in the changing room is a short list of the ten best players to have played for England in their position since 1871 under the title 'One on Us'. This is not meant as an accolade for those on the list but as a source of inspiration for the current incumbent of the jersey. A reminder of those who have gone before them and that no one, not even them, will keep their jersey forever. A recognition that now is their time, their opportunity to write their own name into the annals of English rugby.

The England dressing room.

Accolades

Rugby School caps and jerseys. *Inset*: England cap 1919–20.

Crimson velvet caps were first worn during football matches at Rugby School in the 1830s. By the 1840s stylised jerseys had emerged, bearing the colours and emblems of the side, but the caps endured as a mark of distinction, awarded to those deemed worthy of featuring in Big-Side matches.

Thus began the tradition of awarding caps to selected representative footballers. The tradition became an international convention in 1871 with the awarding of caps to those who took part in the world's first international football match, played, according to rugby rules, between Scotland and England at Raeburn Place in Edinburgh.

Although only a single cap is ever awarded, the number of times a player represents his country is, to this day, referred to as his number of caps.

That first game, won by Scotland in 1871, was initially referred to as simply 'the international contest' but in 1879 the RFU received a trophy from a former club on the Indian subcontinent. Henceforth the Calcutta Cup would be awarded to the winner of the international contest and so became the first achievable accolade for the English national side.

Right: The Calcutta Cup.

Below: England Rugby team, 1871.

Ireland joined the round of annual rugby contests in 1875 – Wales in 1881 – and from at least 1893 onwards writers were compiling tables to represent their overall outcome. The notion of a 'Triple Crown' being awarded to any side that defeated the other three was first referred to in 1894 and established itself as a concept long before the first actual trophy was awarded in 2006.

France officially brought the number of teams involved up to five in 1910 and so instigated the competition that would become known as the 5-Nations Championship. Shared championship victories were commonplace and referred to the situation when two or more teams finished the international season on the same number of points, but would be phased out in 1993 when a trophy was awarded for the first time and tied tables began to be settled on points-difference.

A clean sweep of victories was first described as a Grand Slam in 1957. The achievement now warrants five straight victories since the tournament was expanded to six teams, with the introduction of Italy in 2000.

Triple Crown illustration, 1914.
Inset: Triple Crown trophy.

6 Nations Championship trophy.

Web Ellis trophy.

This book will date the awarding of each of these accolades from the first enabling fixtures rather than from when notions of each were first conceived.

England trophy cabinet, 2014.

1

Loose-head Prop

FREDERIC STOKES (1871-1873)
Birthplace: Greenwich
Position: Forward
Total Caps: 3
Calcutta Cups: 1 (+1 retained)
Triple Crowns: n/a
Outright Championship Victories: n/a
Grand Slams: n/a
World Cups: n/a

In 1871 rugby was still in its embryonic stages but it seems that there was never any real doubt as to who would captain the very first England side. Fred Stokes of Blackheath and Rugby School was an all-rounder, great in the tackle, comfortable in possession and a first-rate drop-kicker. He was known to play at half-back but his constant desire to get his hands on the ball led to him being selected among the forwards. He was the English captain for three consecutive seasons.

Scotland claimed the first international contest but Stokes' side had their revenge the following year. Despite going behind, Stokes' side drew on their mental reserves to fight their way back into the game and eventually secure a 2-1 victory that included three tries.

The 1873 encounter was played on a Glasgow mudbath of a pitch for which Stokes prepared by ordering alterations to the soles of the English boots. These prototype slatted studs helped, but not enough to give his side victory and the contest ended in a 0-0 draw.

At the age of twenty-three, Stokes had played his final international game. He was made RFU President the following year and remains the youngest person to have held the office.

FRANK EVERSHED (1889-1893)

Birthplace: Winshill
Position: Forward
Total Caps: 10
Calcutta Cups: 2
Triple Crowns: 1
Outright Championship Victories: 1
Grand Slams: n/a
World Cups: n/a

Frank Evershed is a test case in the value of experimentation in rugby. Initially a useful three-quarter he was converted into a try-scoring forward on the recommendation of one of his peers. Retaining many of the qualities of a three-quarter, such as rapid acceleration and a swerving gait, he developed a style of play in which he would mercilessly capitalise on opponent's mistakes to create try-scoring opportunities either for himself or his team.

He scored a try in controversial circumstances on his debut against the touring New Zealand Natives side in 1889. He landed another against Scotland the following year, bringing England the Calcutta Cup and ultimately a share of the championship.

He began the 1892 Championship with a try against Wales, helping England on their way in a campaign in which he would be one of the standout performers. Against Ireland, in Manchester, he opened the scoring by outsprinting the Irish backs before setting up a second for his teammate, which settled a close encounter.

He almost landed a third consecutive try against Scotland but England won regardless and Evershed's side had secured an outright championship victory and Triple Crown – their last before the side would be significantly weakened by the events of 1895.

Evershed won ten caps in all.

RAYMOND JOHN LONGLAND (1932-1938)

Birthplace: Lavendon
Position: Prop
Total Caps: 19
Calcutta Cups: 4
Triple Crowns: 2
Outright Championship Victories: 2
Grand Slams: n/a
World Cups: n/a

Ray Longland was one of England's finest props of the interwar years. Strong and heavy he supplied the front-row ballast for England over seven successful seasons in the 1930s.

He made his debut in the final game of the 1932 season, shoring up the scrum and helping secure a Calcutta Cup and share of the Championship. In 1934 he formed a formidable front-row partnership with Gordon Gregory and Henry Rew, helping England complete to a clean sweep of victories, securing the Triple Crown and conceding only 6 points in the process.

He added a victory over New Zealand in 1936 and was a dominant front-row presence during the 1937 season when England swept all before them to claim their second Triple Crown in four seasons.

Longland earned nineteen caps in all. By trade he was a carpenter and he served with the RAF as a PT Instructor during the Second World War.

CHARLES 'THE BADGER' RONALD JACOBS
(1956-1964)
Birthplace: Whittlesey
Position: Prop
Total Caps: 29
Calcutta Cups: 4 (+1 retained)
Triple Crowns: 2
Outright Championship Victories: 3
Grand Slams: 1
World Cups: n/a

At 5 feet 9 inches and 15 stones, Ron Jacobs was almost a custom-built loose-head prop. So comfortable was he near the ground that he soon picked up the nickname 'Badger'. He was described as a forwards' forward – never shirking the grunt work and excelling in loose mauls and tight scrummages.

He made his debut, alongside nine others, in 1956. He then began an unbroken run of thirteen caps during which he helped England win a Grand Slam in 1957 and outright championship victory in 1958. He returned to the side in 1960, helping England to the Triple Crown and was still involved in 1963 when a very different England side claimed another outright championship victory.

The following season he captained England in Paris and Edinburgh to earn the last of his twenty-nine caps.

CLAUDE 'STACK' BRIAN STEVENS (1969-1975)
Birthplace: Godolphin
Position: Prop
Total Caps: 25
Calcutta Cups: 2
Triple Crowns: 0
Outright Championship Victories: 0
Grand Slams: 0
World Cups: n/a

'I don't care if I play left or right as long as I wear an England shirt'.

Cornishman Stack Stevens was versatile enough to play either side of the front row. He made his international debut at the age of twenty-eight after his effective scrummaging and dynamic break-up play in the loose had brought him to the attention of selectors.

His full debut was spectacular – an 11-8 home victory over South Africa, the first time that England had ever triumphed over the Springboks. Victories over southern hemisphere opposition were to become a feature of Stevens' international career. In 1972 he added an away victory over the Springboks and the following year he landed a try to help England on their way to their first ever victory over the All-Blacks in New Zealand. Earlier the same year Stevens had played in every round of a 5-Nations Championship that brought his side a share of the spoils.

Stevens gained the last of his twenty-five caps in 1975 at the age of thirty-five. Away from rugby he was a beef and dairy farmer who attributed his success as a player to his favourite drink … milk.

GARETH 'COOCHIE' JAMES CHILCOTT (1984-1989)
Birthplace: Bristol
Position: Prop
Total Caps: 14
Calcutta Cups: 0
Triple Crowns: 0
Outright Championship Victories: 0
Grand Slams: 0
World Cups: 0

Gareth 'Coochie' Chilcott was an original 1980s skinhead. As a young man he spent his Saturday afternoons following his beloved Bristol City and getting into trouble until a former schoolteacher directed him to his local rugby club where he discovered a more productive outlet for his aggression.

Early in his career the quest to physically dominate his opponents quickly brought him to the attention of numerous officials but he later developed a more rounded game, good in the loose, in line-outs and of course in the scrum, where he was adept in all three front-row positions.

He was first selected for England in 1984 and earned fourteen caps in total. His affable good humour made him an important part of the team and he was selected for the British and Irish Lions in 1989.

When questioned as to what he would do after his retirement he is quoted as saying 'I thought I would have a quiet pint … and about seventeen noisy ones'.

PAUL 'THE JUDGE' ANTHONY GEORGE RENDALL (1984-1991)
Birthplace: London
Position: Prop
Total Caps: 28
Calcutta Cups: 2
Triple Crowns: 0
Outright Championship Victories: 0
Grand Slams: 0
World Cups: Finalist

Paul Rendall, like a fine wine, got better with age. He didn't make his England debut until 1984, at the age of thirty. Having made two appearances Rendall was not selected again until two years later and the following year embarked on an unbroken run that would establish him as an indispensable member of an improving English pack.

Described as one of the best line-out support players in the game, he also brought a calm assurance to the front row. His experience provided a certain authority and earned him the nickname 'The Judge'. He was subsequently appointed judge on numerous overseas tours and on one occasion is reputed to have ordered Brian Moore to wear a dog's collar and drink from a bowl.

In 1987 Rendall helped England reach the quarter finals of the inaugural 1987 Rugby World Cup. He won the Calcutta Cup on two occasions and admitted to having slept with the trophy after retaining it in 1988.

He earned twenty-eight caps in total and remarkably earned the last of these during the 1991 Rugby World Cup, at the age of thirty-seven, helping his side to reach the final in the process.

JASON LEONARD (1990-2004)
Birthplace: Barking
Position: Prop
Total Caps: 114
Calcutta Cups: 11
Triple Crowns: 8
Outright Championship Victories: 7
Grand Slams: 4
World Cups: 1

Early in Jason Leonard's career he was asked to complete a survey by his club, Saracens. He listed 'tackling, scrummaging and strength' as his greatest qualities and the same three attributes as his areas for improvement. Although he described packing down for a scrum as akin to 'being slammed against a wall, with your feet in the air', in the category marked weaknesses he wrote 'not applicable'.

It was this self-belief and stubborn determination that saw him quickly rise to the top of the world game. He began playing as a prop at the age of eleven and throughout his career thrived on the one-on-one confrontation that the position necessitated.

He became England's youngest ever prop forward when making his debut at the age of twenty-one in 1990. He then embarked on a record unbroken run of forty appearances for his country despite suffering serious neck injury in 1992. During this period he helped England to three Grand Slams in 1991, 1992 and 1995 and was a defeated finalist in the 1991 Rugby World Cup.

He remained a regular in the England side during the professional era, adding outright championship victories in 1996, 2000 and 2001, and Triple Crowns in 1997 and 1998. In 2003 he featured in the side that would win another Grand Slam before playing a decisive role in shoring up the English scrum during extra-time of the 2003 Rugby World Cup Final, which England went on to win.

On taking the field he said to the referee 'you know me, I go forwards, I go backwards, I don't go up and I don't go down so you won't be getting any penalties'.

The ultimate team player, on learning that another had been selected ahead of him the first thing that Leonard would do was pass on all he knew about the opposition.

By the time he retired he had amassed a record 114 caps during an international career that spanned the amateur and professional eras and included two World Cup Finals.

He is the most decorated player in the history of English rugby.

GRAHAM 'WIG' CHRISTOPHER ROWNTREE
(1995-2006)
Birthplace: Stockton
Position: Prop
Total Caps: 54
Calcutta Cups: 5
Triple Crowns: 5
Outright Championship Victories: 3
Grand Slams: 2
World Cups: Semi-finalist

'I've always had a burning desire to play for my country. Always have done and always will'.

Graham Rowntree's power and fearless scrummaging brought him to the attention of selectors in 1993 when he was first selected for an England squad. He would have to wait another two years to make his debut, which came in time for him to help England to a Grand Slam in 1995.

Later that year he featured in the group stages of 1995 Rugby World Cup that would see England progress to the semi-finals. The following year Rowntree was promoted to first choice loose-head prop and helped England achieve a second consecutive outright championship victory.

A Triple Crown followed in 1997, and further appearances in the 1999 World Cup, before Rowntree was left out of the squad in 2000. With twenty-six caps and a string of international accolades it would have been reasonable to expect him to call time on his international career at this point; Rowntree however hadn't finished.

As the game changed so did he, adding running and handling to his game and achieving continual success with his club side Leicester Tigers. In 2001 he returned to the international set-up and put in a man of the match performance in a 21-15 victory against Australia.

He added a Triple Crown in 2002 and a Grand Slam in 2003. He earned the last of his fifty-four caps in 2006, thirteen years after being first selected for a squad.

A respected scrum technician, Rowntree has been an England forwards coach since 2007. Of his position he says, 'Keep your discipline and they will eventually lose theirs.'

ANDREW JOHN SHERIDAN
(2004-2011)
Birthplace: Bromley
Position: Prop
Total Caps: 40
Calcutta Cups: 2
Triple Crowns: 0
Outright Championship Victories: 1
Grand Slams: 0
World Cups: Finalist

Andrew Sheridan first appeared on the radar when trampling all over his opponents with Dulwich College. At 6 feet 5 inches he was initially a lock, but soon moved into the front row where his strength and frame could inflict the most damage.

He helped England U18s to a Grand Slam in 1998 and made his full debut as a substitute in 2004. In 2005 he made his first start for England and announced his arrival as an international Test rugby player by annihilating the Australian front row and helping England to a 26-16 victory.

Two years later Sheridan solidified his reputation as one of the most feared scrummagers in the world by repeating the performance in the quarter finals of the 2007 Rugby World Cup. His man of the match performance against Australia delivering a bruising 12-10 victory and facilitating England's run to the final.

In 2009 Sheridan made his first Test start for the British and Irish Lions, helping them to a Test victory against South Africa. In 2011 Sheridan helped England claim their first outright championship victory since 2003. Later that year he earned the last of his forty caps during the 2011 World Cup.

2

Hooker

CHARLES GURDON (1880-1886)
Birthplace: Barnham Brook
Position: Forward
Total Caps: 14
Calcutta Cups: 3 (+2 retained)
Triple Crowns: 2
Outright Championship Victories: 2
Grand Slams: n/a
World Cups: n/a

Charles Gurdon and his brother Edward Temple were the standard bearers for 1880s English rugby. As well as two magnificent moustaches the pair brought solidity, work-rate and commitment to the side for almost a decade.

Charles led the forwards from the front in a ceaseless, untiring, always powerful and always dangerous style. Although heavy he was also clever with his feet and, like a racehorse, was described as being 'quick over dry ground'.

He earned the first of his fourteen caps in 1880 and was made captain during the 1882 season. In 1883 and 1884 he helped his side to back-to-back Triple Crowns during a dominant period for English rugby. In 1884 he was described as 'equal to, if not better than, any other forward to have played in England'.

He and his brother earned their final caps in 1886, retaining the Calcutta Cup in the process.

ROBERT LIONEL SEDDON (1887)
Birthplace: Salford
Position: Forward
Total Caps: 3
Calcutta Cups: 1 retained
Triple Crowns: 0
Outright Championship Victories: 0
Grand Slams: n/a
World Cups: n/a

Bob Seddon was the only player to have been described as being 'good at every point of the game' in Lillywhite's 1886 *Football Annual*. Elsewhere the versatile broad-shouldered forward was described as 'one of the best forwards in the north' and a 'typical Lancashire lad'.

Seddon lost both his parents at an early age and had grown up an operative in the manufacturing districts of Manchester. Off the field, as well as on it, he was respected as a sportsman and a gentleman.

He had earned three England caps in 1887, retaining the Calcutta Cup in the process, and it seems likely that he would have gone on to win more due to his hardworking, determined but fair approach on the field.

In 1888, he was elected by his teammates to be the first ever captain of a side that would go on to become the British and Irish Lions. He scored three tries on the tour but was tragically killed in a sculling incident on the Hunter River in New South Wales.

NORMAN ATHERTON WODEHOUSE
(1910-1913)
Birthplace: Basford
Position: Forward
Total Caps: 14
Calcutta Cups: 2
Triple Crowns: 1
Outright Championship Victories: 2
Grand Slams: 1
World Cups: n/a

The word 'hero' is often freely bandied about in relation to sport but Norman Wodehouse was a hero in every sense of the word.

Born in Basford, by the age of fifteen he had enrolled in the Royal Naval College and was selected to represent them in 1907. A line-out specialist, Wodehouse was marked out by his ability to lead and inspire at an early age both on and off the field.

He earned his first England cap against France in 1910 and went on to help his side to a first outright championship since 1892. He was an ever-present force in the side over the next two seasons and was promoted to captain at the end of the 1912 season.

The following year he became the first English captain to lead his side to a clean sweep of victories – an achievement now known as a Grand Slam.

Wodehouse had made history and will forever be remembered as England's first Grand Slam-winning captain, but his life achievements were only just beginning.

By the outbreak of the First World War Wodehouse had achieved the rank of Gunnery Officer and was posted to the HMS *Revenge*, which became engaged in the Battle of Jutland. After the battle he received a medal for having left his own ship to save the life of a drowning seaman who had fallen overboard from a different vessel.

Wodehouse remained with the Royal Navy after the war and was promoted to Commander. By the time of his retirement in 1940, he had attained the rank of Admiral. The Second World War cut short his retirement and he returned to take command of a convoy heading south along the western coast of Africa.

When the convoy came under attack from German U-boats he ordered them to scatter, saving many lives but sadly not his own.

JOHN SAMUEL TUCKER (1922-1931)
Birthplace: Bristol
Position: Hooker
Total Caps: 27
Calcutta Cups: 1
Triple Crowns: 1
Outright Championship Victories: 2
Grand Slams: 1
World Cups: n/a

Sam Tucker was the first in a rich line of Bristol hookers to have represented England. An honest scrummager, described as 'invaluable' by his former captain William Wavell Wakefield, Tucker matured into the type of front-row forward that spread confidence throughout the pack.

Tucker had fought during the First World War and been wounded at the Battle of the Somme with the Royal Engineers.

He made his international debut in a cameo performance against Wales in 1922 but wasn't selected again until the visit of the All-Blacks in 1925. The appearance foreshadowed an unbroken run in the side that continued into the 1929 season.

In 1928 he scored a try in an international against New South Wales and helped his side to a clean sweep of five victories that delivered his first, and England's fourth, Grand Slam of the 1920s.

Tucker's most remarkable season however was possibly 1930. While not initially selected, at the age of thirty-four he was called up as a late replacement and flown across the Bristol Channel. There he helped England to an away win at Cardiff Arms Park. By the end of the season he had been instated as captain and England duly won the Championship.

Tucker earned the last of his twenty-seven caps in 1931 at the age of thirty-five.

ERIC EVANS (1948-1958)
Birthplace: Droylsden
Position: Hooker
Total Caps: 30
Calcutta Cups: 5
Triple Crowns: 2
Outright Championship Victories: 3
Grand Slams: 1
World Cups: n/a

Eric Evans credits his success as a rugby player to his father who, from an early age, fostered within him the type of mental resilience that would make him a future England captain. He also bequeathed him a professional approach to training that would lead Eric to spend part of the 1950s training with Matt Busby's Manchester United side.

Evans was a schoolteacher, born in Droylsden, who played for Old Aldwinians and Sale. He was first selected for England in 1948 and earned the first of his thirty caps as a loose-head prop against Australia. By 1953 Evans had become a regular in the side, in his favoured position of hooker, and was a member of the unbeaten 1953 side who won that year's Championship.

He was dropped from the side in 1955 before being reinstated as captain in 1956 at the age of thirty-four. In 1957 he led England to their first Grand Slam since 1928, followed by an undefeated outright championship in 1958.

Evans was a no-nonsense, combative player on the pitch who led by example. In the dressing room he was feted for his rabble-rousing, blood and thunder pep talks. But away from the pitch he was the life and soul of every party, placing a premium on team spirit and camaraderie. He never underestimated the importance of togetherness among his teammates and described rugby, years later, as being '90% psychology'.

JOHN VIVIAN PULLIN (1966-1976)
Birthplace: Aust
Position: Hooker
Total Caps: 42
Calcutta Cups: 5
Triple Crowns: 0
Outright Championship Victories: 0
Grand Slams: 0
World Cups: n/a

At a time when England had little success north of the equator, hooker John Pullin enjoyed considerable success against formidable opponents in the south. A farmer by trade, Pullin was appreciated by his teammates for his cool head and wry, self-deprecatory wit.

His international career lasted more than ten years and included a then record fourty-two caps. He notched his one and only try in the final stages of a game against South Africa in 1969, earning England her first ever victory against the Springboks.

Three years later, on receiving the captaincy, Pullin led England to another victory against the South Africans, this time 18-9 in Johannesburg. In 1973 he added New Zealand and Australia to his list, beating the All-Blacks 16-10 in Auckland before demolishing the Wallabies 20-3 at Twickenham.

He would record further victories against the All-Blacks with the Barbarians and twice with the British and Irish Lions.

In 1972 Scotland and Wales cancelled their visits to Dublin on account of the political situation there. England showed no fear as Pullin led them out the following season and, despite losing 18-9, Pullin managed a smile, remarking, 'we're not much good but at least we turn up'.

PETER JOHN WHEELER (1975-1984)
Birthplace: South Norwood
Position: Hooker
Total Caps: 41
Calcutta Cups: 4 (+2 retained)
Triple Crowns: 1
Outright Championship Victories: 1
Grand Slams: 1
World Cups: n/a

Peter Wheeler made his first appearances in the white jersey in 1971 as part of an England XV tour of the Far East. There he helped secure victories over Japan, Hong Kong and Singapore. But he would have to wait until 1975 before earning his first full cap in place of long-serving hooker John Pullin.

The following season Wheeler cemented his place in the side by winning four strikes against the head and helping England to a 23-6 victory over Australia. In 1980, with Fran Cotton and Phil Blakeway, he spearheaded a front row that dominated all of England's 5 Nations opponents and delivered a first Grand Slam since 1957.

Wheeler earned the last of his forty-one caps in 1984 but not before he had captained the side to a memorable 6-3 victory over New Zealand at Twickenham in 1983.

During rugby's professional age Wheeler has maintained his association with the sport as chief executive of Leicester Tigers.

BRIAN 'PITBULL' CHRISTOPHER MOORE (1987-1995)
Birthplace: Birmingham
Position: Hooker
Total Caps: 64
Calcutta Cups: 7 (+1 retained)
Triple Crowns: 3
Outright Championship Victories: 3
Grand Slams: 3
World Cups: Finalist

Brian Moore is remembered as a ferocious competitor who psychologically outfought opponents on the biggest stage. He was no stranger to the dark arts of front-row scrummaging but his tactical awareness and ability to marshal his teammates in the face of provocation elevated him beyond his contemporaries.

He made his debut in 1987, helping England avoid the wooden spoon with a Calcutta Cup victory over Scotland. By 1990 he had Jeff Probyn and Jason

Leonard either side of him in a front row that supplied a platform of stability for what would become the most feared pack in world rugby.

In response to the disappointment of 1990, Brian Moore's skills were to fore the following year as England sought to control the field and their opponents. It worked and a Grand Slam was secured. A similar approach was adopted later in the year and helped England reach the final of the 1991 Rugby World Cup. A second Grand Slam followed in 1992 and, in 1995, Moore's final season, a third before the veteran helped England to the semi-finals of the 1995 Rugby World Cup.

A combative player on the field, he was equally so off it and became a forthright defender of players' rights as the game moved towards professionalism.

He retired having played in sixty-four out of seventy-two international fixtures over a period of eight years. Since then he has become a respected, insightful and often outspoken broadcaster.

MARK 'RONNIE' PETER REGAN (1995-2008)
Birthplace: Bristol
Position: Hooker
Total Caps: 47
Calcutta Cups: 3
Triple Crowns: 2
Outright Championship Victories: 3
Grand Slams: 1
World Cups: 1

Mark Regan took up rugby at the age of eight and there was only ever one position for him. As a youngster he idolised Brian Moore, and it must have been with a great sense of pride that he succeeded Moore as England hooker in 1995.

The following year he helped England to a Triple Crown and outright championship. A further Triple Crown followed in 1997 before Regan lost his place in the team early in the 1998 campaign.

Persistence however was to be the key to Regan's career and he worked his way back into the squad in time to help England to an outright 6 Nations Championship in 2001. Another absence followed before a cameo appearance helped England to a Grand Slam in 2003 and later that year a try-scoring contribution in the group stages of the tournament earned Regan a winner's medal at the 2003 Rugby World Cup.

With these achievements under his belt Regan retired from international rugby in 2004. But three years later, at the age of thirty-five, he forced his way back into the side in the run-up to the 2007 World Cup. Against all the odds he retained his place in the side and embarked on a campaign that would take England all the way to the final. He is remembered as one of the standout performers in England's crucial quarter-final victory against Australia.

He earned the last of his forty-seven caps in 2008 at the age of thirty-seven.

STEVEN THOMPSON (2002-2011)
Birthplace: Hemel Hempstead
Position: Hooker
Total Caps: 73
Calcutta Cups: 5 (+1 retained)
Triple Crowns: 2
Outright Championship Victories: 2
Grand Slams: 1
World Cups: 1

Steve Thompson joined Northampton Saints as a flanker but Ian McGeechan wanted him at the front so he added 13 pounds to his 6-foot-2-inch frame and converted to hooker. He didn't lose all of his back-row attributes however; his pace, handling and ball carrying setting him aside from his rivals.

So effective was he that he was fast-tracked into the England team at the start of the 2002 season and essentially remained there for five years until injury restricted his involvement.

In his first year he helped England to a Triple Crown. In 2003 he scored a try against Italy to help England to a Grand Slam and another against Georgia during the 2003 Rugby World Cup, which Thompson and England would go on to win.

In 2004 Thompson endured only his second defeat in twenty-five caps. In 2007 he suffered a serious neck injury that appeared to have ended his career. However within ten months he had returned for his club side. Speaking about his decision to return his £500,000 insurance payout he remarked 'I don't regret it…it was just about playing rugby'.

Two years later he returned for the national side and would earn an additional twenty-five caps.

His substitute appearances helped England to an outright championship in 2011 and his final appearance came in the quarter finals of the 2011 Rugby World Cup.

He played seventy-three times for England in total.

The 1892 Team

The RFU County Championship became a regular part of the English rugby calendar in 1889. It was a roaring success and reflected the popularity of county representative rugby that would soon attract crowds in excess of 30,000. County rugby helped grow the profile of the sport nationwide and it wasn't long before it began to have a material impact on the composition of the England team.

What the tournament showed beyond all doubt was that one English region in particular was pre-eminent. Of the first nine County Championship finals, Yorkshire won eight. The other was won by Lancashire. This phenomenon can partly be explained away by numbers. Lancashire and Yorkshire combined represented one of the most densely populated regions in Western Europe. But the type of player that sprang from the urban manufacturing centres of the two counties was quite different from the gentleman amateurs that had so far characterised the game.

England v Wales illustration, 1892.

Dicky Lockwood was a woollen printer from Crigglestone. His introduction of the three-quarter system and darting runs, from what would become outside centre, paved the way for the creative attacking play of Yorkshire and later England. He received his international call-up at the age of nineteen and his successful introduction to the side opened up a seam of northern talent.

Among these was broad-shouldered Bob Seddon who had worked in the manufacturing districts of Manchester and Salford since he was a child. In 1888 Seddon would become the first captain of a side that is now known as the British and Irish Lions.

Part-way through the 1890 season England suffered a chastening defeat at the hands of Yorkshire and the influx of working-class players into the national side intensified. No fewer than five were selected among the forwards alone for that season's Calcutta Cup, including Jack Toothill, a licensee from Bradford.

These players, allied to stalwarts such as Frank Evershed and Sammy Woods, improved English fortunes and the side won that year's Calcutta Cup and claimed a share of the Home Nations Championship.

This process of democratisation within the England team reached its nadir in 1892 with a side that included colliers, iron moulders, builders, publicans, printers and railway traffic agents as well as solicitors and schoolteachers. The approach paid dividends as England, under the captaincy of strategist Fred Alderson, recorded a clean sweep of victories.

1892 England v Ireland dinner menu.

England v Ireland, 1890.

The season began with a comprehensive 17-0 drubbing of a strong Welsh side at Rectory Field. Lockwood orchestrated the English backs and put in one of his finest performances contributing a try and two goals for his side.

The second match would be played against Ireland at Whalley Range in Manchester. This time it was a much tighter affair but Evershed and Woods combined well to make the difference as England ran out 7-0 winners.

England's final game represented their sternest challenge. Scotland, the reigning champions, had been the strongest of the home nations for several years and you would have to go back to 1884 to find a season in which they hadn't at least shared victory in the tournament. The game would be played at Raeburn Place, Edinburgh and Scotland began as strong favourites.

With the Yorkshire forwards to the fore the English pack turned the screw. A fiercely combative encounter, typified by mauling and sporadic violence, was secured by a narrow 5-0 margin.

England's class of 1892 had won the championship, Calcutta Cup and Triple Crown and had done so without conceding a single point. This unique feat has never been matched by any England side either before or after 1892.

England v Wales, 1892.

England v Scotland, 1892.

3

Tight-head Prop

SAMUEL MOSES JAMES WOODS (1890-1895)
Birthplace: Ashfield
Position: Forward
Total Caps: 13
Calcutta Cups: 2
Triple Crowns: 1
Outright Championship Victories: 1
Grand Slams: n/a
World Cups: n/a

Born in the suburbs of Sydney, Sammy Woods didn't arrive in England until the age of sixteen. Thereafter he quickly began to practise and excel at sport. In 1888 he was selected to represent England at cricket. Two years later he earned a call-up for rugby and went on to captain the national side in 1892.

Although included here as a forward he was equally at home among the backs. He was famous for quick breaks and relentless dribbling. A teammate described him as a 'demon in the tight-scrums and loose mauls' who 'ran with the fury of a charging rhino'. His tackling was so effective that another contemporary described being tackled by Woods as akin to being hit by a motor car.

England claimed a share of the Championship during Woods' first international season in 1890. In 1892 Woods was awarded the captaincy and landed a conversion while helping England defeat Ireland on their way to a first Triple Crown since 1884.

He earned the last of his thirteen caps in 1895.

Woods served as a military sensor in Sudan at the age of fifty during the First World War.

JOHN 'THE PROPHET' DANIELL (1899-1904)
Birthplace: Bath
Position: Prop
Total Caps: 7
Calcutta Cups: 1
Triple Crowns: 0
Outright Championship Victories: 0
Grand Slams: n/a
World Cups: n/a

John 'The Prophet' Daniell was England's inspirational, but sadly often absent, captain in the opening years of the twentieth century.

Between 1899 and 1907 England finished bottom of the Championship table six times. What difference might Daniell, whose work often made him ineligible for selection, have made?

When Daniell did play he led the forwards with tremendous heart, desire and vigour. A natural leader, he had an intuitive understanding of the scrum and ability to foster team spirit. When he was not there his absence was always felt.

He played seven times for his country. He was captain in all but one of his appearances and was one of the few English players of his generation to retire with a positive win record. His understanding of the game was later put to good use as a selector.

His approach to the scrum was 'shove, shove, shove until the enemy is shoved right off the ball, leaving it all alone for your scrum-half to pick up, and take home to his Aunt Fanny if he wishes'.

WILLIAM GEORGE ERNEST LUDDINGTON (1923-1926)
Birthplace: Ashfield
Position: Prop
Total Caps: 13
Calcutta Cups: 2
Triple Crowns: 2
Outright Championship Victories: 2
Grand Slams: 2
World Cups: n/a

'Magnificent Luds' was a regular in some of England's most successful sides of the 1920s. His captain, William Wavell Wakefield, who favoured stout broad-shouldered front-row forwards, described him as being 'splendidly proportioned', and his powerful shoulders were also eulogised by a former England scrum-half who also praised his 'boundless energy' and 'bulldog' spirit.

But Luddington had technical skills too and, at a time when England had no recognised kicker, would regularly step up to the mark to score points for his side.

He made his debut at the start of the 1923 season and won eight consecutive games with the side, claiming back-to-back Grand Slams in the process. In his first season he converted a try in the dying moments of the game against Scotland, at Inverleith, to hand England a narrow 8-6 victory. He added another in the final game against France.

In 1925 he managed three conversions, a penalty and a goal from a mark, scoring more than half of his side's 13 points at Stade Columbes. He also became the first international player to score at Murrayfield by landing a penalty in that famous stadium's opening fixture.

He earned the last of his thirteen caps in 1926, retiring with an 85 percent win record. Away from the field he served with the Royal Navy on board aircraft carrier HMS *Illustrious*. By the time the Second World War broke out in 1939 he had reached the rank of master-at-arms.

Engaged in the Mediterranean, HMS *Illustrious* came under attack from German dive-bombers in 1941. Although the ship survived the attack, she suffered severe casualties, her master-at-arms among them.

Devenport RFC named one side of Rectory Field 'the Luddington Memorial Stand' in his memory.

MICHAEL ALAN BURTON (1972-1978)
Birthplace: Maidenhead
Position: Prop
Total Caps: 17
Calcutta Cups: 1
Triple Crowns: 0
Outright Championship Victories: 0
Grand Slams: 0
World Cups: n/a

'Natural desire' was how Mike Burton summed up his uncompromising and often brutal approach to rugby. Nothing summed up his 'never stay down' attitude better than him playing against France and Wales with a broken jaw in 1974. His performances in these two fixtures helped him to be selected for the 1974 Lions, whose unbeaten tour of South Africa represented the pinnacle of his career.

Born in Maidenhead he was first selected in 1972 and earned seventeen caps before representing England for a final time in 1978. His international career coincided with lean years for England but he helped his side to wins over South Africa in 1972 and Australia in 1978.

FRANCIS 'FRAN' EDWARD COTTON (1971-1980)
Birthplace: Wigan
Position: Prop
Total Caps: 31
Calcutta Cups: 4
Triple Crowns: 1
Outright Championship Victories: 1
Grand Slams: 1
World Cups: n/a

Fran Cotton had the strength and technical skill to play at either tight-head or loose-head prop and did so thirty-one times for his country in total. At 6 feet4 inches he was tall for his position, but his strength and raw commitment made him a dangerous asset.

He was involved in notable victories over New Zealand and Australia in 1973. Earlier the same year he helped England to five-way-split success in the 5 Nations Championship.

At the end of the 1977/78 season it seemed that Cotton's international career had come to an end but after helping a the Northern Division demolish New Zealand in 1979 he was recalled.

In his final season Cotton would prove to be the cornerstone of a formidable English pack that would go on to claim England's first Grand Slam since 1957. It was a fitting reward for a player who had represented his country with distinction throughout the 1970s.

After retiring Cotton retained his association with the game as an administrator and was the team manager of the British and Irish Lions during their successful tour of South Africa.

GARY STEPHEN PEARCE (1979-1991)
Birthplace: Dinton
Position: Prop
Total Caps: 36
Calcutta Cups: 2 (+2 retained)
Triple Crowns: 0
Outright Championship Victories: 0
Grand Slams: 0
World Cups: Finalist

Gary Pearce made his first mark on international rugby when flattening England's Fran Cotton during a training match at Bisham Abbey. Cotton was out for the first two games of the 1978 season and Pearce was picked up by Northampton Saints. A year later the quiet unassuming front-row forward had taken Cotton's place in the England team, playing in every round of the 1979 season.

It was the start of an international career that would span three decades, ending with Pearce as England's most capped forward of all time.

Perhaps the most memorable of his thirty-six caps came in 1983 when Pearce lined up against the visiting All-Blacks. Within ten minutes he had lost an ear; he returned to the field and received a broken nose for his trouble. Despite this Pearce saw out the game and England won.

Pearce helped his side to the quarter-finals of the inaugural Rugby World Cup in 1987 but was only selected once the following season. Three years later he returned to earn his final cap during the 1991 Rugby World Cup.

JEFFREY ALAN PROBYN (1988-1993)
Birthplace: Bethnal Green
Position: Prop
Total Caps: 37
Calcutta Cups: 4 (+1 retained)
Triple Crowns: 2
Outright Championship Victories: 2
Grand Slams: 2
World Cups: Finalist

To Jeff Probyn, punches were a badge of honour. If he was getting hit then it was generally because his team was winning.

Probyn's disruptive, sloped-shouldered scrummaging technique posed a riddle that few managed to solve and wrought havoc in northern-hemisphere rugby for years. Agile and a good tackler, he was also strong, despite claiming to have never visited a gym.

But possibly the most remarkable thing about Probyn's career is that he earned the first of his thirty-seven caps in 1988 at the age of thirty-one. 'Age is all in the mind' he said. 'If you're good enough, then you're young enough.'

He was rarely out of the side over the following six seasons, a period during which he helped England to a World Cup Final and back-to-back Grand Slams in 1991 and 1992. He played his final game for England in 1993 at the age of thirty-six.

JULIAN WHITE (2000-2009)
Birthplace: Plymouth
Position: Prop
Total Caps: 51
Calcutta Cups: 3
Triple Crowns: 2
Outright Championship Victories: 2
Grand Slams: 1
World Cups: 1

Julian White was a self-confessed country boy. Work as a dairy farmer took him to New Zealand and Wales and developed his rugby career along the way. By the time he made his England debut in 2000 he had established a reputation as a destructive yet technically gifted scrum specialist.

His preference for fronting-up necessitated a level of aggression that sometimes boiled over but he described this mean streak as a necessary part of his game: 'I cannot dilute my aggression or passion.'

An appearance against France in 2001 helped England secure an outright championship and White added a Triple Crown the following year.

Another appearance against France contributed to a Grand Slam in 2003 and White then appeared in the group stages as England went on the seal the 2003 Rugby World Cup.

White was a regular in the side until the end of the 2007 6-Nations. He returned to the side for a further seven caps in 2009, earning fifty-one caps in total.

Towards the end of his career his wife bought him a cow for Christmas. It turned out to be a portent. Since retiring White has returned to dairy farming.

PHILIP 'RAGING BULL' JOHN VICKERY (1998-2009)
Birthplace: Barnstaple
Position: Tight-Head Prop
Total Caps: 73
Calcutta Cups: 4
Triple Crowns: 2
Outright Championship Victories: 2
Grand Slams: 0
World Cups: 1

It is entirely appropriate that a Cornish cattle farmer from Devon should earn the nickname Raging Bull. A tightly controlled ball of aggression, Phil Vickery was surprisingly mobile for someone of 20 stone and 6 feet 3 inches.

His skill in the scrum was apparent early on: 'there are small blokes, big blokes, fat blokes, thin blokes; you've got to learn to deal with them all'. His combative nature is summed up by a tattoo on his arm, the Japanese kanji for which roughly translates as 'fight to the death'.

England secured a Triple Crown in his first season as an international. Outright championship wins followed in 2000 and 2001 before another Triple Crown in 2002. In 2003 Vickery helped England to back-to-back away wins over Australia and New Zealand before playing in every single match of a tournament that would deliver his side the 2003 Rugby World Cup.

He would captain England for the first time in 2002. In 2007 he was made permanent captain of the side and led England to another World Cup Final later that year.

He played his last game for England in 2010 having amassed seventy-three caps – fifteen as captain.

MATTHEW STEVENS (2004-2012)
Birthplace: Durban
Position: Prop
Total Caps: 44
Calcutta Cups: 2
Triple Crowns: 0
Outright Championship Victories: 0
Grand Slams: 0
World Cups: Finalist

'When I go onto the pitch I want to absolutely annihilate them in the scrum. That's how I feel about the game and if I haven't done that then I'm disappointed with myself'.

Matt Stevens was born and raised in Durban and only came to England to study at Bath University. His scrummaging and mobility were quickly noticed by the local rugby club and English parentage meant that his future lay with the red rose.

He was first selected for England in 2004. In 2007 he helped England reach the final of the Rugby World Cup.

In 2009 Stevens received a two-year ban after having tested positive for a controlled substance. After demonstrating considerable remorse Stevens was offered the chance to rebuild his career at Saracens before making an improbable charge for inclusion in England's 2011 Rugby World Cup squad.

Stevens helped England reach the quarter-finals of the tournament before earning the last of his forty-four caps in 2012.

4

Lock

MURRAY WYATT MARSHALL (1873-1878)
Birthplace: Guildford
Position: Forward
Total Caps: 10
Calcutta Cups: 2 (+ 2 retained)
Triple Crowns: n/a
Outright Championship Victories: n/a
Grand Slams: n/a
World Cups: n/a

At a time when rugby games featured twenty players per side and often turned into fierce wars of attrition with endless scrums, Murray Marshall was worth his weight in gold. Described as the best tight-scrummager of his day, his personal resolution, work rate and commitment were often the factors that decided the outcome of international contests.

Marshall, described as a 'capital tackler, with plenty of dash', had a relentless hunger for possession and was described as the hardest worker in the English side.

He made his debut in 1873, helping England retain the Calcutta Cup in his first game. He went on to help his side either win or avoid defeat against Scotland over four consecutive seasons. His total of ten consecutive caps over six seasons was an English record that stood for thirty-six years.

JOHN 'JACK' THOMAS TOOTHILL (1890-1894)
Birthplace: Thornton
Position: Forward
Total Caps: 12
Calcutta Cups: 2
Triple Crowns: 1
Outright Championship Victories: 1
Grand Slams: n/a
World Cups: n/a

England lost their first game of the 1890 Home Nations Championship and then lost comprehensively to Yorkshire, who had established themselves as the champion county in English rugby. It was therefore clear where salvation lay.

For England's next game five Yorkshiremen were selected among the English forwards, including Jack Toothill.

Toothill was a 'dashing', pacey forward who specialised in making breaks and causing problems for the opposition. He was also a master of the long-forgotten art of dribbling and is reported to have once taken the ball three quarters of the length of the field in this fashion.

The selection of Toothill and the Yorkshire contingent was vindicated when England claimed the Calcutta Cup and won their remaining fixtures without conceding a try. This was enough to earn a share of the championship and laid the foundations for English rugby's first period of forward dominance.

Another victory to nil came against Ireland in 1891 with Toothill contributing one of his side's five tries. The ongoing successes of the Yorkshiremen presaged an influx of working-class talent that would fundamentally alter the make-up of the national side.

In 1892 the policy paid off in nines. Four tries gave England a 17-0 victory against Wales, followed by two further victories to nil against Ireland and Scotland. England had landed their first clean sweep since 1883 and had done so without having conceded a single point.

Toothill remained with the England side until 1894, earning twelve caps in total. Away from the field he was a publican in Bradford and his native Thornton. After the 1895 schism he and nine other members of the famous 1892 side would cross the divide by becoming professional Rugby League players.

GEOFFREY SEYMOUR CONWAY (1920-1927)

Birthplace: Cardiff
Position: Lock/Flanker/Hooker
Total Caps: 18
Calcutta Cups: 4
Triple Crowns: 3
Outright Championship Victories: 3
Grand Slams: 3
World Cups: n/a

Rugby was in Geoffrey Conway's blood. Although he later became an archaeologist, at the time of his glittering international career he was a schoolmaster at Rugby School. A versatile forward, Conway could play in the first, second and back rows and earned the nickname 'Prince of the Dribblers' for his skilful footballing skills that were a greater feature of the game in the 1920s than they are now.

Conway was awarded a Military Cross in 1917 and was one of twenty-one players to make their England debut in 1920, as play resumed following the First World War.

He played in the final game of the 1921 Grand Slam winning season and took on responsibility for kicking conversions the following year. In 1923 and 1924 Conway played in every game, kicking a then record seven conversions in 1924 and helping his side to back-to-back Grand Slams.

He returned for his final cap in 1927, earning eighteen in all.

RONALD 'COVE'-SMITH (1921-1929)
Birthplace: Edmonton
Position: Lock
Total Caps: 29
Calcutta Cups: 5
Triple Crowns: 4
Outright Championship Victories: 4
Grand Slams: 4
World Cups: n/a

Throughout the 1920s Ronald Cove-Smith was the backbone of one of the most successful English packs to have taken the field before or since. Described by his 1924 captain William Wavell Wakefield as 'dogged, thorough and solid', Cove-Smith was in the thick of every maul, wearing down and demoralising his opponents with his incessant work rate. He made particular use of his strength in wheeling and driving the scrum towards the touchline, a move that was then legal and deprived the opposition of quick ball.

He made his debut halfway through the 1921 season, helping England to away wins against Scotland and France and securing a first Grand Slam since before the First World War. After missing the opening game of the 1922 season he then embarked on a run of sixteen consecutive caps across a period that secured two further Grand Slams in 1923 and 1924.

By 1925 he had amassed thirteen England caps without having lost a single game. In 1928 much of that earlier Grand Slam-winning side had gone, but Cove-Smith remained. He was made captain and duly surpassed many of his peers by delivering a fourth Grand Slam the same year.

Away from the field Cove-Smith was medical practitioner; he never smoked and remained a teetotaller for all of his eighty-eight years.

JOHN 'MUSCLES' DAVID CURRIE (1956-1962)
Birthplace: Clifton
Position: Lock
Total Caps: 25
Calcutta Cups: 3 (+ 2 retained)
Triple Crowns: 2
Outright Championship Victories: 2
Grand Slams: 1
World Cups: n/a

John Currie began life as a centre but by the time he had been selected for England in 1956 he had graduated into the complete second-row forward. Currie had the distinction of being the powerhouse in an English pack that at the time was the most formidable that England had ever assembled.

In 1957 he helped England to a first Grand Slam for almost thirty years. An outright championship victory followed the next season and a shared victory and Triple Crown in 1960.

Although his nickname was 'Muscles', Currie had far more than strength about his game. He was a skilful ball-carrier and outstanding jumper and, in his debut international season, even kicked four penalties. His second-row partnership with David Marques is to this day a combination that has never been bettered.

He earned twenty-five England caps and played club rugby until the age of thirty-seven.

ROGER MILES UTTLEY (1973-1980)
Birthplace: Blackpool
Position: Lock
Total Caps: 23
Calcutta Cups: 4 (+ 1 retained)
Triple Crowns: 1
Outright Championship Victories: 1
Grand Slams: 1
World Cups: n/a

At 6 feet 4 inches Roger Uttley was a natural in the second row. Effective at the lineout, with good balance, he made his Test debut in 1973 and helped England to a first away victory over New Zealand and home victories against France, Scotland and Australia in the same year.

Uttley's form saw him selected for the 1974 British and Irish Lions tour of South Africa. But, at a time when the lineout more closely resembled a mass brawl than a set piece, Uttley also possessed the destructive skills required to make life difficult for opponents. This, allied to his speed and mobility around the pitch, saw him switched to blindside flanker for all four tests, from which the Lions emerged unbeaten.

Uttley was moved into the back row for England in 1975 and captained the side four times in 1977 as a No. 8. In 1980, his final international season, Uttley was moved to blindside flanker and emulated his feats with the Lions by helping England to their first Grand Slam since 1957.

He retired with twenty-three caps but later returned to the Lions and England set-up as a coach and manager during the 1980s and 1990s.

WILLIAM BLACKLEDGE BEAUMONT (1975-1982)
Birthplace: Preston
Position: Lock
Total Caps: 34
Calcutta Cups: 4 (+ 2 retained)
Triple Crowns: 1
Outright Championship Victories: 1
Grand Slams: 1
World Cups: n/a

Bill Beaumont was first selected for England in 1975, halfway through England's worst decade since the 1900s. He soon impressed with his combative, blood-and-thunder brand of rugby that seemed to the perfect antidote to the frustration felt by many England fans at the time. By the end of the year he had embarked on an unbroken run of appearances for the national side that would last eight years.

Beaumont's leadership qualities were there for all to see and he was first made England captain in 1978. In 1979 he lead a North of England representative side to a comprehensive victory against the visiting All-Blacks and made the bold prediction that his improving side would not only win the following years' 5 Nations Championship, but that they would do so by claiming the Triple Crown.

England hadn't outright won a championship since 1963 or the Triple Crown since 1960 but over four gruelling contests, including a nail-biting 9-8 victory over a Welsh side that had dominated the 1970s, Beaumont was proven correct.

He retired due to injury in 1982 but not before he had captained the national side a then record twenty-one times. In doing so he had also become England's most capped lock with thirty-four caps in total.

PAUL JOHN ACKFORD (1988-1991)
Birthplace: Hanover
Position: Lock
Total Caps: 22
Calcutta Cups: 1 (+1 retained)
Triple Crowns: 1
Outright Championship Victories: 1
Grand Slams: 1
World Cups: Finalist

Perseverance is a word that well characterises Paul Ackford. He threatened to break into the England side at the age of twenty-one when selected for the B side, but instead would have to wait until he was thirty before finally getting the call-up in 1988.

Tall and mobile, Ackford believes that it was the resurgence of these qualities in the second row that made the difference.

His debut came against Australia in 1988, a game that England won and set England on the road to one of their most successful periods. In 1991 Ackford played in every round of a 5 Nations campaign that brought England a first Grand Slam since 1980. Later the same year he helped England to the 1991 Rugby World Cup Final.

The final at Twickenham would be the last of Ackford's twenty-two caps.

MARTIN OSBORNE JOHNSON (1993-2003)

Birthplace: Solihull
Position: Lock
Total Caps: 84
Calcutta Cups: 9
Triple Crowns: 6
Outright Championship Victories: 4
Grand Slams: 2
World Cups: 1

Martin Johnson was concussed for most of his 1993 international debut. The fact that he was singled out as having shored up the English lineout and ensured a narrow victory over France was indicative of the type of impact he would go on to have for his team.

At 6 feet 7 inches and 18 stone Johnson was England's colossus, but his quiet manner off the field belied a burning ambition on it. While other players lost their heads in the heat of battle, Johnson constantly got on with the job of winning ball, driving his team forwards and controlling the pitch to the advantage of his team.

As a youngster he went to learn his trade in New Zealand where he received tutoring from Colin Meads. He impressed and was selected to represent the New Zealand Colts, after which Meads personally guaranteed that Johnson's future lay with the All-Blacks. He was wrong.

On earning his second England cap, Johnson helped his side to their first victory over New Zealand in ten years. He became a regular in the side over the following season and helped England to a Grand Slam in 1995.

A natural leader, Johnson became captain of England in 1999, two years after he had successfully lead the British and Irish Lions on their tour of South Africa. Outright championship victories were secured in 1996, 2000 and 2001.

In 2003 Johnson would captain England during English rugby's most successful season. A dominant Grand Slam was secured after Johnson's immovable side racked up five tries in Dublin during a 42-6 win. That summer Johnson led his side to back-to-back wins over New Zealand and Australia before taking England to the 2003 Rugby World Cup in Australia.

Leading by example throughout the tournament, his driving run helped set-up Jonny Wilkinson's last-minute drop-kick to secure a 20-17 win in the final in Sydney. His last act as captain was to become the first Englishman to lift the Webb Ellis Cup.

In 2009 Johnson was declared England's Player of the Century by public vote and with characteristic modesty he attributed the accolade to the 2003 team rather than himself as an individual.

In 2011 Johnson coached England to another outright championship victory, England's first since 2003.

Martin Johnson as England manager, 2009.

SIMON DALTON SHAW (1996-2011)
Birthplace: Nairobi
Position: Lock
Total Caps: 71
Calcutta Cups: 4
Triple Crowns: 2
Outright Championship Victories: 3
Grand Slams: 1
World Cups: 1

Simon Shaw was born in Nairobi and grew up in Spain. Consequently he didn't come into contact with a rugby ball until he was seventeen. Two years later he was selected for England.

But Shaw's meteoric rise does not adequately reflect his long England career. The key word for the 6-foot-9-inch lock would instead be persistence.

Although selected to tour South Africa in 1994, Shaw didn't earn his first cap until 1996. The following year he helped England to a Triple Crown before another period of absence from the side. He returned in 2000 and England became outright champions.

Another absence followed before Shaw helped England to a Grand Slam in 2003. Later that year he would join up with the squad that would eventually claim the 2003 World Cup.

Despite earning his medal Shaw was denied the opportunity of playing in the showcase tournament until 2007, when at long last his persistence finally paid off. An integral component of a pack that would lead England to a second consecutive World Cup final, Shaw would start in all but one match of England's 2007 Rugby World Cup campaign.

Having been selected for three consecutive British and Irish Lions squads, Shaw finally made his Test debut against South Africa in 2009.

In 2011 Shaw helped England to another outright championship before playing his final game in the quarter finals of the 2011 World Cup.

He retired seventeen years after having been first selected for England, having earned seventy-one caps.

The 1913-1914 Team

In 1910, after a generation of mediocrity, Adrian Stoop at long last led England out of the post-1895 malaise. In doing so he fundamentally altered the English approach to rugby, adopting the 'two half back system' that we now understand as the distinction between the positions of fly-half and scrum-half. In addition he pioneered a free-spirited attacking game, utilising backs as well as forwards. These innovations were enough to deliver a long-awaited championship but also laid the foundations for the truly special team that would follow.

Among the backs Stoop championed his Harlequins/Oxford University teammate and Rugby School alumni Ronnie Poulton, who debuted in 1909 at the age of nineteen. A try scorer and provider with a swerving gait, Poulton epitomised Stoop's attacking game and it wasn't long before he was making eye catching contributions to the side.

England v France, 1913.

Further forward, another player had also realised that England would have to change their style to compete. Cherry Pillman had watched Dan Gallaher as a boy and developed his game in succeeding years to become England's first recognised wing-forward.

Elsewhere in the pack the diminutive Jack King, Australian-born Bruno Brown and Jenny Greenwood would make sure that the opposition were never given a moment's respite in possession.

Above: England v Scotland illustration, 1913.

Below: England v Wales, 1914.

In 1913 this developing group came together under the inspired leadership of Norman Wodehouse, whose calm strategy and mastery of the pack sent England into the field with confidence.

Before the championship season could begin England would meet a touring South Africa side and two promising youngsters; fly-half Dave Davies and wing Kid Lowe were given their debuts. They immediately suffered a bloody nose in a 9-3 reverse but it would turn out to be a useful baptism of fire. Indeed it would be the first and only time that Davies would taste defeat in an international career that spanned eleven years, either side of the First World War.

It was Davies' quick hands that set up Vincent Coates for England's first try of the 1913 5 Nations campaign. Coates would play for a single season but his try was the first of six in four games. Elsewhere Pillman was a constant menace and prevented the Welsh from finding a rhythm before adding a try of his own to give England a 12-0 victory and their first victory in the principality since 1895.

Six tries were shared between Coates, Poulton and Pillman as England despatched France 20-0 a week later before the team headed to Dublin. This time the English pack terrorised the Irish defence allowing Pillman, Coates and John Ritson to go over four times for a 15-4 victory.

The season's final game was a much closer affair but once again the English pack were on hand to rule the roost over the visiting Scots and Bruno Brown went over for the only score of the match. Wodehouse had delivered English rugby's first Grand Slam without conceding a single try.

Wodehouse himself was unavailable the following year and so Ronnie Poulton became England captain in advance of his fourteenth international appearance. The captaincy had always been, and remains, a crucial aspect of English selection. It is a responsibility to which some players rise and Poulton was about to do so admirably.

The absence of Wodehouse and King meant that the English pack would not be quite so dominant in 1914 and England looked instead to the creativity of their backs. The approach suited Poulton, who delivered two quite brilliant performances in the opening two fixtures that included a narrow 10-9 home victory against Wales and 17-12 home win over Ireland.

England on the attack against France, 1913.

England v France, 1913.

Perhaps inspired by his captain, Davies contributed a memorable solo run in which he beat three Irish players before touching down. Lowe, meanwhile, had had a season to bed in and would now embark on a devastating run of form that began with two tries against the Irish.

These were heady days for English rugby with six straight wins for the first time since the 1880s. A classic encounter was to follow in Inverleith. Lowe continued his run of form with a hat-trick of tries either side of the break and Poulton, who had set impossibly high standards for himself, added one of his own. Scotland however managed three tries of their own and the match finished with England securing the Triple Crown by a whisker – 16-15.

This set England up for a grandstand finish in Paris. Lowe scored another hat-trick of tries to finish the tournament with eight, an English record that has never been beaten. Jenny Greenwood was imperious with the boot kicking six conversions and Poulton, now operating on a level denied to mere mortals, scored four tries in what would prove to be his final international appearance.

In contrast to the shackled forward-driven side of 1913 Ronnie Poulton's England had scored twenty tries in three games, thus becoming the first English side to claim back-to-back Grand Slams.

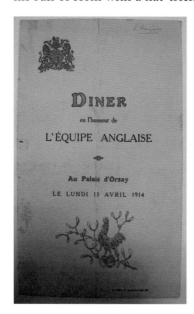

England v France dinner menu, 1914.

5

Lock

LEONARD 'BRUNO' GRAHAM BROWN (1911-1922)
Birthplace: Brisbane
Position: Forward
Total Caps: 18
Calcutta Cups: 4
Triple Crowns: 3
Outright Championship Victories: 3
Grand Slams: 3
World Cups: n/a

Bruno Brown personified the move towards mobile front men that played a large part in English rugby's dominant period during the 1920s. Historically forwards had relied on power to drive the ball into the opposition's half but Brown preferred to pass and run. His teammate William Wavell Wakefield commented that Brown's preference for getting the ball quickly away from the lineout encouraged his teammates to adopt a more open passing game.

Brown made his debut against Wales in 1911. He then played in every game of England's back-to-back Grand Slams of 1913 and 1914 and it was his try against Wales in the final game of the 1913 season that gave England their first. After the war he was recalled to the England side and scored tries against Ireland and Scotland in helping England to another Grand Slam in 1921. He earned eighteen caps in total, winning in fourteen of them.

During the First World War he served with the Royal Army Medical Corps. He received the Military Cross in 1917 and was mentioned in despatches the following year. In later years he assisted in the foundation of the Australian Rugby Football Union in 1949.

KENDRICK JAMES STARK (1927-1928)
Birthplace: Edmonton
Position: Lock
Total Caps: 9
Calcutta Cups: 1
Triple Crowns: 1
Outright Championship Victories: 1
Grand Slams: 1
World Cups: n/a

K. J. Stark earned nine caps over two seasons and was generally regarded as being England's most effective player in the loose. His defensive skills were allied to technical ability, which he demonstrated by assuming kicking duty in the 1927 Calcutta Cup contest, in which he landed a penalty and conversion.

The following year in Swansea and Dublin he would be called upon to marshal his side in appalling conditions typified by wind, mud and rain. Stark led from the front, his two magnificent defensive displays helping deliver narrow wins for his side.

The achievement left England requiring home wins against France and Scotland. These were duly delivered and England claimed a Grand Slam that was bolstered by a capped victory against New South Wales earlier in the season.

Stark would serve with the Royal Army Service Corps in the Second World War and was mentioned in despatches.

REGINALD WILLIAM DAVID MARQUES (1956-1961)
Birthplace: St Margarets
Position: Lock
Total Caps: 23
Calcutta Cups: 3 (+ 2 retained)
Triple Crowns: 2
Outright Championship Victories: 2
Grand Slams: 1
World Cups: n/a

David Marques was always very clear as to who inspired his participation in the sport. His father was his 'absolute inspiration in everything'.

At 6 feet 5 inches Marques towered over almost all of his competitors and quickly came to achieve absolute mastery of the lineout. In all but one of the twenty-three consecutive international games he played for his country he was paired with John Currie in the famed Marques-Currie axis – a second-row combination that has never been bettered.

Marques and Currie debuted against Wales in 1956 and were motivated to succeed by a newspaper that criticised them as being 'too inexperienced' on the morning of their first game. For the next five years the duo formed the engine room of the finest pack in the northern hemisphere.

A first Grand Slam in almost thirty years was delivered the following season, followed by an outright championship victory in 1958. In 1960 Marques would score the winning try in a home victory over Ireland that would allow England to seal that year's Triple Crown.

MAURICE JOHN COLCLOUGH (1978-1986)
Birthplace: Oxford
Position: Lock
Total Caps: 25
Calcutta Cups: 3 (+1 retained)
Triple Crowns: 1
Outright Championship Victories: 1
Grand Slams: 1
World Cups: n/a

Maurice Colclough apparently had to cut holes in the sides of his socks to get them on over his prodigious calf muscles. Fran Cotton described him as 'the strongest scrummager I ever came across'. At 6 feet 4 inches with flaming ginger hair and beard, Colclough was always a noticeable presence for England during his twenty-five caps, which began with a win over Scotland in 1978.

In 1980 he solidified his place in the team alongside Bill Beaumont, his power in the scrum and driving runs a key factor in three victories that brought England a first Grand Slam since 1957.

Further highlights of an international career that spanned eight seasons include a win over Australia in 1982 and a try against New Zealand in 1983 that secured a first home win against the All-Blacks since 1936.

WADE ANTHONY DOOLEY (1985-1993)
Birthplace: Warrington
Position: Lock
Total Caps: 57
Calcutta Cups: 5 (+1 retained)
Triple Crowns: 1
Outright Championship Victories: 2
Grand Slams: 2
World Cups: Finalist

Blackpool policeman Wade Dooley was working night-shifts when he received his first international call up. It took him some time to adapt to training sessions that were effectively in the middle of the night. Adapt he did however and his 6 feet 8 inches commanding lineout presence and reliability in the scrum earned him the nickname the 'Blackpool Tower' as well as fifty-seven caps.

His white headband, with a strip of black tape through the middle, became a regular feature of the England team from his England debut in 1985 until he retired in 1993, a period which included back-to-back Grand Slams and a World Cup Final.

On receiving his call-up he had the following advice for his fellow players:

It really is a wonderful thing to be able to say that I have played rugby for my country. I know a lot of players on the brink of representative selection get discouraged and think that their chance will never come. But I can only say to them all, stick at it, good luck and remember, dreams do come true. Mine certainly did because even in my wildest dreams I never imagined January 1st, 1985 would be the day my life changed forever.

MARTIN CHRISTOPHER BAYFIELD (1991-1996)
Birthplace: Bedford
Position: Lock
Total Caps: 31
Calcutta Cups: 4
Triple Crowns: 3
Outright Championship Victories: 3
Grand Slams: 2
World Cups: Semi-finalist

In the late amateur era 6 feet 4 inches was actually quite short for a lock. Fortunately for Martin Bayfield he had reached that height by the age of twelve. By the time he turned out for England for the first time in 1991 he was 6 feet 10 inches and remains the tallest player ever to have taken the field in a red rose.

Before turning professional Bayfield, like several of his teammates, was a policeman. At a time when lineout laws were changing, his towering presence was a key weapon in the English pack armoury.

In 1992 he starred in every game of England's Grand Slam-winning season, helping England to their first back-to-back Slam since 1924. In 1995 he secured another Grand Slam for his side and went on to play in the semi-final of the 1995 Rugby World Cup.

He added another outright championship and Triple Crown in 1996 before retiring from the game with thirty-one caps.

GARATH STUART ARCHER (1996-2000)
Birthplace: Durham
Position: Lock
Total Caps: 21
Calcutta Cups: 2
Triple Crowns: 2
Outright Championship Victories: 2
Grand Slams: 0
World Cups: Quarter-finalist

'I won't take a backward step be it a rugby or a physical challenge. Whether it's a tackle, a scrum, or fisticuffs I won't come second.'

Garath Archer took up rugby at the age of fourteen and realised his childhood dream of playing for England in 1996 at the age of twenty-one.

A solid scrummager, technically strong and fiercely competitive, in his first cap he helped England win the Calcutta Cup. Then, in his first full season, he claimed the Triple Crown and an outright championship.

In 1998 he secured a second Triple Crown by helping England to wins against Wales, Ireland and Scotland. The following year he started two games in the 1999 Rugby World Cup, a campaign that would end at the quarter-final stage.

In 2000 he replaced Martin Johnson in the national side and helped England to another outright championship. He earned twenty-one caps in total. After retiring at the age of twenty-nine he took up rowing and became a British Indoor Rowing champion in 2009.

DANIEL JONATHAN GREWCOCK (1997-2007)
Birthplace: Coventry
Position: Lock
Total Caps: 69
Calcutta Cups: 8
Triple Crowns: 3
Outright Championship Victories: 2
Grand Slams: 1
World Cups: 1

Danny Grewcock was reputed to be ninth in line when he received his first call-up for the national side. Most first choice players were away with 1997 British and Irish Lions. But he didn't let this prevent him from putting in a try-scoring debut and so lay out his credentials for permanent inclusion.

Grewcock was a relative latecomer to rugby but his skill in the lineout and preference for mobile running rugby allowed him to progress swiftly.

The following year he featured in a campaign that brought England the Triple Crown. He played four times in the 1999 Rugby World Cup before helping England to an outright championship in 2001 and another Triple Crown in 2002.

He was a consistent contributor to England's 2003 Grand Slam and also played a part in the 2003 Rugby World Cup success, although injuries limited his appearances.

In 2004 he assumed Martin Johnson's berth in the side and earned a total of sixty-nine caps before his retirement in 2007.

BEN JAMES KAY (2001-2009)
Birthplace: Liverpool
Position: Lock
Total Caps: 62
Calcutta Cups: 4
Triple Crowns: 2
Outright Championship Victories: 1
Grand Slams: 1
World Cups: 1

Ben Kay came through at a time when England had enormous strength in depth in the second row. Despite this his rise was meteoric. Initially a lineout specialist, with a knack for stealing opposition ball, he would add ball-carrying and big tackles to his game as he learned from the example of his Leicester Tigers second row teammate Martin Johnson.

Clive Woodward was keen to replicate the partnership at international level and Kay received his first call-up in 2001. The following year Kay and Johnson linked up for the 6 Nations and duly delivered a Triple Crown before helping England to successive wins against New Zealand, Australia and South Africa.

In 2003 Kay played in every round of a Grand Slam-winning season before helping his side to back-to-back away wins against New Zealand and Australia. He was then first choice partner to Johnson as England won the 2003 Rugby World Cup in Sydney.

In a little over two years since making his debut Kay had won every accolade in international rugby. He would feature for his side in each the next six seasons and in 2007 he drove his side to a second successive World Cup Final.

On completing his final game in 2009 he had accumulated sixty-two caps in total.

STEVEN WILLIAM BORTHWICK (2001-2010)
Birthplace: Carlisle
Position: Lock
Total Caps: 56
Calcutta Cups: 2 (+1 retained)
Triple Crowns: 0
Outright Championship Victories: 1
Grand Slams: 0
World Cups: Finalist

Mike Tindall described Steve Borthwick as 'the nicest man in the world off the field' but a 'nightmare' on it. As a player Borthwick was initially a lineout specialist but grew into a dogged man-of-war characterised by leadership and intelligence.

He made his England debut against France in 2001, helping England to an outright championship at the age of twenty-one. In 2003 he was selected for the provisional World Cup squad but he didn't begin to feature regularly for England until 2004.

Borthwick played in the group stages of the 2007 Rugby World Cup, helping England to the final in the process. In 2008 he was installed as England captain, an honour he fulfilled twenty-one times until his final cap in 2010. In all he represented his country fifty-six times and said of the experience,

It really is a privilege to play for your country. I look back and think I gave the very best I could and worked as hard as I could to put in a performance that does the jersey proud and does the England team proud.

6

Blind-side Flanker

WILLIAM 'PUSHER' YIEND (1889-1893)
Birthplace: Winchcombe
Position: Forward
Total Caps: 6
Calcutta Cups: 1
Triple Crowns: 1
Outright Championship Victories: 1
Grand Slams: n/a
World Cups: n/a

Pusher Yiend was a late bloomer and made his international debut against the touring New Zealand Natives side in 1889 at the age of twenty-seven. England won in controversial circumstances but, despite playing well, Yiend was not selected for the following two seasons.

In between he continued to develop his game. He would come to be regarded as one of the finest protagonists of the art of cover defending, single-handedly halting his opponent's rush before his teammates could arrive in support.

His cool head saw him promoted to captain of his side Hartlepool Rovers and he was selected as a founding representative of the Barbarians in 1890.

He returned to the England side in 1892, adding some much needed ballast to the English scrum. 1892 would be a season of emphatic success in which Yiend and his side would claim the Home Nations Championship, the Calcutta Cup and Triple Crown without conceding a single try. The season would prove to be England's only outright championship victory in a period that would span for twenty-seven years.

Yiend earned the last of his six caps the following season aged thirty-one. Away from rugby he was a railway worker.

CHARLES 'CHERRY' HENRY PILLMAN (1910-1914)
Birthplace: Sidcup Hill
Position: Flanker
Total Caps: 18
Calcutta Cups: 4
Triple Crowns: 2
Outright Championship Victories: 3
Grand Slams: 2
World Cups: n/a

As a boy Cherry Pillman is purported to have been present when the 1905 touring All-Blacks took on England at Crystal Palace. If true it would seem that while everyone else was becoming irate at the borderline infringement play of New Zealand captain Dan Gallaher young Charles was taking notes.

A few years later he would become one of a select few English rugby players to have effectively reinvented his role in the team. He not only adopted Gallaher's spoiler tactics but added several more tricks to his arsenal. His speed allowed him to be the first away from the scrum whereupon his athleticism allowed him to fix upon the opposition ball carrier and mercilessly exploit any errors. So successful was he in this role that he quickly became a regular instigator of his side's attacking play.

He forced his way into the England team after having demolished an England-elect side in a final 'Probables v Possibles' trial match in the run-up to Twickenham's inaugural international fixture in 1910. Once in the side he proved his worth, cementing his place and helping England to a first Championship success since 1892.

A golden period followed. Pillman scored tries in 1911 and 1912 before being one of the stand-out performers in the 1913 Championship. Tries against Wales, France and Ireland helped earn a first English Grand Slam.

1914 would be the final season before the outbreak of war but Pillman was at the very peak of his powers. He landed a match-winning try to give England a narrow victory against Wales and scored another to help defeat Ireland. The following game would be Pillman's last and ended with him being carried from the field with a broken leg. His brother Robert replace him for the final game of the season in which England secured a second consecutive Grand Slam by beating France.

During the First World War Pillman served with the 4th Royal Irish Dragoon Guards and added a Military Cross to his eighteen international caps. His brother Robert sadly perished at the Somme. After the war he would return to Twickenham as captain of the 'Mother Country' during the King's Cup of 1919.

ANTHONY THOMAS VOYCE (1920-1926)
Birthplace: Gloucester
Position: Flanker
Total Caps: 27
Calcutta Cups: 5
Triple Crowns: 3
Outright Championship Victories: 3
Grand Slams: 3
World Cups: n/a

Tommy Voyce was ever to be found in the heat of the battle. He enjoyed the physical aspects of the game so much that open aggression from his opponents would likely as not earn them a cheerful grin in return. His persistent good humour earned him the nickname Happy Warrior, although the Welsh preferred to call him the Grinning Menace.

Voyce however was not just a smiling face. He was technically proficient enough to play anywhere across the back-row and in 1924 played with distinction at full-back, centre and wing for the British and Irish Lions.

He received his England call-up in 1920 at the outset of a period of outstanding success for the national side. He played in every game of the Grand Slam seasons of 1921, 1923 and 1924 securing a total of twenty-seven caps before his final outing in 1926.

Away from the field Voyce served in the army during the First World War and as a major during the Second World War. He was President of the RFU from 1960–61 and would receive an OBE for his services to sport before passing away at the age of eighty-three.

DONALD FREDERICK WHITE (1947-1953)
Birthplace: Earls Barton
Position: Flanker
Total Caps: 13
Calcutta Cups: 4
Triple Crowns: 0
Outright Championship Victories: 1
Grand Slams: 0
World Cups: n/a

Much is made today of the English white-wall of defence, a tradition that can be traced back to one appropriately named man. When asked about the composition of his team Don White replied, 'I want fifteen tacklers. If you knock them all down, they can't get back up.'

He was first selected in 1947 and helped his side to a share of the Championship. An archetypal hard man, strong, with good hands and a powerful kick, he was venerated by his teammates for his character and leadership as well as his uncompromising approach to defence.

However, his strong-arm ways were not to everyone's taste and England's opponents were mystified to see White omitted from the national side during the 1949, 1950 and most of the 1951 season. After losing the opening three games of the 1951 season he was recalled and answered his critics by scoring the match-winning try against Scotland.

A prolonged run in the side then resulted in a six-game unbeaten run that brought White and England the 1953 5 Nations Championship.

In all White won thirteen caps. In 1969, in recognition of White's deep understanding of the sport, he became the first man to coach the national side.

PETER GEORGE DEREK ROBBINS (1956-1962)
Birthplace: Coventry
Position: Flanker
Total Caps: 19
Calcutta Cups: 3 (+2 retained)
Triple Crowns: 2
Outright Championship Victories: 2
Grand Slams: 1
World Cups: n/a

Peter Robbins was a blessing and a curse to his teammates. His explosive shoves from the back row added weight to the scrum but often left his teammates with bruised thighs. His barn-storming runs expressed his natural attacking flair but he was also impossible to shift once locked onto loose ball.

Robbins made his debut at the start of the 1956 season alongside nine others in a new-look side. The following year the side clicked and England secured their first Grand Slam since 1928. They won the championship again in 1958. Wholesale changes were made in 1960 but Robbins retained his place and helped England to the Triple Crown.

In all Robbins earned nineteen caps. He described rugby as 'a strong drink to be slipped slowly and in the company of true friends'.

MICHAEL GORDON SKINNER (1988-1992)
Birthplace: Newcastle upon Tyne
Position: Flanker
Total Caps: 22
Calcutta Cups: 2
Triple Crowns: 1
Outright Championship Victories: 1
Grand Slams: 1
World Cups: Finalist

Micky Skinner was one of the game's last great amateurs. He disliked training so much that he regularly considered giving up the game towards the end of the off-season. Fortunately for England he was consistently talked around and his fully committed, maximum impact tackling quickly established him as one of the game's most feared competitors.

He earned the first of his caps in 1988 in an era when England were blessed with talented back-row specialists. Alternating with the likes of Teague, Winterbottom and Richards, he nailed down his position in the side during the 1991 Rugby World Cup.

Skinner is remembered to this day for his emphatic tackle on Marc Cecillon in an ill-tempered quarter-final against France. Late in the game as the English pack were forced to resist wave after wave of French pressure; Skinner's decisive intervention helped turn the contest England's way.

He continued his enforcer role through to the World Cup Final and into the following season when he helped England secure a second consecutive Grand Slam.

Despite playing at the highest level Skinner stayed true to his amateur roots throughout his career, mixing with fans and enjoying a drink in the public lounge after a game.

In all he earned twenty-two caps.

MICHAEL CLIVE TEAGUE (1985-1993)
Birthplace: Gloucester
Position: Flanker
Total Caps: 27
Calcutta Cups: 2 (+1 retained)
Triple Crowns: 1
Outright Championship Victories: 1
Grand Slams: 1
World Cups: Finalist

'Strong in the arm' was how many described Mike Teague, who was a builder by trade. It was probably this quality that earned him the nicknames 'Popeye' and 'Iron Mike', as much as his all-round power, athleticism and constant desire to drive the ball forwards.

Teague made his international breakthrough in 1985 but was then seemingly discarded. His absence from the national side lasted for three years, during which time he took up weightlifting before converting from a No. 8 to blind-side flanker. He returned to the England fold at the age of twenty-eight.

In 1991 he scored a try against Wales, helping England to their first win in Cardiff in twenty-eight years and, later, to their first Grand Slam since 1980. Later that year he would help England reach a World Cup Final.

The following year Teague played in a win against South Africa before earning the last of his twenty-seven caps in 1993.

TIMOTHY ANDREW KEITH RODBER (1992-1999)
Birthplace: Richmond
Position: Flanker
Total Caps: 44
Calcutta Cups: 5
Triple Crowns: 4
Outright Championship Victories: 3
Grand Slams: 2
World Cups: Semi-finalist

Tim Rodber believed that your first duty as a No. 6 was to make a nuisance of yourself. This he did, as well as being effective in the loose and a lineout ball winner. He was also a proponent of big tackles and a shrewd decision maker, calling on reserves of physical and mental strength honed by a professional career in the army.

His first cap at the age of just twenty-two allowed him a walk-on part in England's 1992 Grand Slam season. By 1994 he had established a more permanent presence in the back row and helped his side to another Grand Slam in 1995 and the semi-finals of the 1995 Rugby World Cup. He then featured in campaigns that earned his side an outright championship in 1996 and Triple Crown in 1997.

In 1998, after more than a decade in the back row, Rodber was converted into a second-row lock-forward and helped secure a victory against world champions South Africa.

He went on to amass forty-four caps in all and made his final appearances during England's 1999 Rugby World Cup campaign.

RICHARD ANTHONY HILL (1997-2004)
Birthplace: Dormansland
Position: Flanker
Total Caps: 71
Calcutta Cups: 6
Triple Crowns: 3
Outright Championship Victories: 3
Grand Slams: 1
World Cups: 1

Richard Hill began playing rugby at the age of five. As a senior his progress was rapid. Quick, offering constant support for the backs, it wasn't long before some were comparing him to the likes of Peter Winterbottom.

He was first introduced to the England set-up in 1997. Within six months he had helped them to win the Calcutta Cup and Triple Crown and starred on the successful 1997 British and Irish Lions tour of South Africa.

He spent time as an open-side flanker and No.8 before Clive Woodward picked him at blind-side, thus solving the puzzle of England's back row. Alongside Lawrence Dallaglio and Neil Back, Hill formed one third of what would become known as the Holy Trinity, England's finest ever back-row combination.

Initially Hill was the quiet member of this trio but would surpass both his teammates in terms of tackling and work rate. His ability to break with the ball also saw him gaining yards and scoring tries.

In 2000 and 2001 Hill scored tries on the way to outright championship victories but the Grand Slam eluded him and his team. In 2003 it duly arrived and Hill helped England to back-to-back away wins over Australia and New Zealand before succumbing to an injury that threatened to rule him out of the 2003 Rugby World Cup.

However, Hill was the only player never to be dropped by Clive Woodward during England's most successful period. He returned to the starting fifteen in time for England's semi-final with France. A week later he helped England to become the first northern hemisphere side to lift the Webb-Ellis Cup.

He continued to play at international level until 2004 and scored his twelfth try, against Australia, during the last of his seventy-one caps.

JOE PAUL RICHARD WORSLEY (1999-2011)
Birthplace: London
Position: Flanker
Total Caps: 78
Calcutta Cups: 6 (+1 retained)
Triple Crowns: 3
Outright Championship Victories: 4
Grand Slams: 1
World Cups: 1

Joe Worsley's goal was always simple: 'to be one of the best players in the world', and this would be a necessary prerequisite of breaking into a side that contained the likes of Dallaglio, Hill, Back and Moody as options in the back row.

Worsley, at 6 feet 5 inches, had a deceptively low centre of gravity and was as useful on the ground as he was destructive around the field. His power, strength and endurance also meant that he very rarely waned even in the most competitive of environments.

He made his international debut in the group stages of the 1999 Rugby World Cup and made a sufficiently good impression to remain in and around the squad as England became 6 Nations champions in 2000 and 2001 and Triple Crown winners in 2002.

As competition for places intensified Worsley's frequently outstanding performances ensured that he would remain in contention. His try against Wales helped England to a Grand Slam in 2003 and contributions in the group stages helped England win the 2003 Rugby World Cup.

Four years later he played in every round of the 2007 Rugby World Cup, helping England to the final with a last-ditch tap tackle against France in the semi-final.

He continued with the squad until 2011 when he was involved in another Championship-winning side. He amassed seventy-eight caps in total, scoring ten tries.

The 1921-1924 Team

In total England lost twenty-seven international players during the First World War, including captain Ronnie Poulton and five others who had played in the final game against France before the outbreak of hostilities in the summer of 1914.

Several former players did return however, including flanker Jenny Greenwood who was selected as captain of the national side when international rugby finally resumed in 1920. Among the others were Kid Lowe, the flying winger, and Gloucester flanker Sydney Smart.

England lost their first game but were shored up in the second by the return of fly-half Dave Davies. Davies had been one of England's most influential players in 1914. Now, aged twenty-nine, the skilful veteran demonstrated that he would be crucial to the fortunes of his side by landing the only try in a narrow victory against France.

Further victories were added against Ireland and Scotland to earn a share of that year's Championship and over the course of the season the team was improved by the introduction of several new faces who, collectively, would form the core of next great England side.

Geoff Conway, Freddie Blakiston, Tommy Voyce and William Wavell Wakefield were all versatile athletic forwards who could play in a number of positions. Conway was perhaps the most versatile of all, playing initially as a hooker but later in the second and back rows. Blakiston was a tireless chaser who specialised in hunting down opponents and applying pressure to opposition ball carriers.

Voyce had the technical skills and awareness to play among the backs but relished the confrontation of the pack so much that he preferred to remain where the action was. Wakefield, as well as making the hard yards, was a master tactician whose revolutionary forward play would shortly reap huge dividends for his side.

In the backs came Eddie Myers and Alistair Smallwood while Cecil Kershaw was fast developing a useful partnership with Davies at scrum-half.

One other player returned to the fold at the start of 1921. Bruno Brown had first debuted in 1911, before helping England to Grand Slams in 1913 and 1914. Now aged thirty-two, he would bring stability to the front-row, allowing the younger men to cut loose in the rear.

Only Wales had beaten England in 1920 but the new look, fast-developing England side demolished the men in red by four tries to one in the opening game of the 1921 season. Since Greenwood had retired, Davies had been promoted to captain and relished in the role of creator, combining with Kershaw and Myers to handsome effect.

Lowe contributed his fourth try in four games, against Ireland, as England raced to a 15-0 victory. Brown, enjoying his return to international rugby, scored a try in that game and added another in an 18-0 victory against Scotland in Inverleith, which brought Davies' side the Triple Crown.

A tall, rangy lock called Ronald Cove-Smith made his debut in this game and a further addition arrived ahead of the final game in Paris in the shape of fast, creative centre Len Corbett. The game against France was tightly contested but first-half tries from Blakiston and Lowe, plus controlled defensive kicking from Davies, were enough to give England the win and a first Grand Slam of the interwar period.

Wales v England match programme, 1924.

England v Wales match ticket, 1923.

England v Ireland, 1927.

England now had a mostly settled side but stout front-row forward John Tucker was brought in for the first of his caps at the start of the 1922 season. Disaster then struck in the shape of an injury to Davies prior to the opening game against Wales. Brown was promoted to captain in his place but bemoaned the privilege in a private letter to Davies in which he said that he would 'gladly have foregone the honour to have had you in your place in the team'. The importance of the fly-half to the side was reaffirmed as England lost to Wales in his absence.

Davies returned and was reinstated as captain for the second fixture and England were undefeated for the remainder of the season. More ballast was added to the side at the start of the 1923 season in the shape of prop Bill Luddington and, barring any unexpected injuries, it was hoped that the side might emulate the feats of 1921.

England not only had key personnel in every position, they also had considerable faith in each other. In Cove-Smith's memoirs he recalls his teammates pulling down the windows of their train and cheering as they pulled into Peterborough Station to collect Blakiston and then doing the same at Grantham as they collected Smallwood. The England side of 1923 was not just a collection of rugby players but a happy band of brothers.

They began the 1923 season playing into a Twickenham gale which inadvertently gifted them a try within 10 seconds of kick-off. Wakefield's kick

England, 1921.

blew into the hands of Leo Price who attempted a dropped goal. Instead of landing the points the ball blew back into Price's hands and the flanker ran in for a try as the Welsh searched the skies for the ball!

Wales equalled the scoring shortly after but the game was settled by an audacious dropped goal from Smallwood from just inside the halfway line and touch.

England followed up this narrow victory by demolishing Ireland by five tries to one at Welford Road. Meanwhile Scotland had beaten France, Wales and Ireland and so England's next match would decide a Triple Crown as well as a Calcutta Cup. The Scots had home advantage and a strong side of their own and led a close encounter with 15 minutes remaining.

England however kept their cool. Harold Locke, earning his first cap, then intercepted a loose ball before booting up field. Voyce

Scotland v England match programme, 1921.

collected for the try, pulling England level before Luddington calmly converted to give England the win.

With the Triple Crown secured England went to Paris in search of a clean sweep. This would be their captain's final international game and, with the fixture already settled by tries from Conway and Voyce, Davies bowed out by landing a dropped goal with the final play off the game. Wakefield later insisted that Davies had deliberately planned this show-stopping finale and such was the fly-half's skill that he might well have done.

Davies' career, along with Kid Lowe's, had spanned either side of the First World War and included four Grand Slams. His scrum-half partner Kershaw also bowed out having played fourteen times with Davies and having never lost a game. To this day Davies and Kershaw are statistically England's most effective half-back partnership.

With these three influential players retiring, 1924 was expected to be a season of rebuilding for England but as it turned out the side had significant strength in depth. Carston Catcheside was brought in to replace Lowe and Arthur Young came in at scrum-half while Myers was moved from the centres to replace Davies at fly-half.

There was never any doubt as to who would replace Davies as captain. W. W. Wakefield was a natural leader who's tactical mastery of the forwards and heroic head-first drives, ball in hand, were synonymous with all of the teams in which he played. His teammates had absolute faith in him and hopes were high. Unfortunately his first game as captain would be against Wales in Swansea, where England hadn't won since 1895.

Wales scored first but were subsequently undone by searing interplay from the newly configured English backs. Tries from Myers, Jake Jacob and Locke followed to give England the lead. In the second half the onslaught continued with two tries from Catcheside. Voyce suffered a broken rib early in the half but played on till the end, helping secure a 17-9 victory in the process.

A trip to Belfast followed and a fiercely contested game against Ireland that was locked at 3-3 with 70 minutes played. England however finished with a flurry of tries, the last of which, a length of the field score from Catcheside, gave England a 14-3 victory.

A comfortable home victory against France followed meaning that for the second consecutive season the Calcutta Cup match would settle the outcome of the season. This time England were rampant. Their captain Wakefield opened the scoring himself before second half tries for Catcheside and Myers gave England a 19-0 victory and a second consecutive Grand Slam.

Instead of rebuilding, Wakefield's side had secured a third English Grand Slam in four seasons, a feat that no other side has matched either before or since. Over seven seasons England had won four Grand Slams.

But the roaring twenties weren't over. Wakefield continued until 1927 and Ronald Cove-Smith took over as captain the following year. With the help of Tucker, Young, Carl Aarvold and Kendrick Stark, Cove-Smith added a fourth and final Grand Slam to see out the decade.

England v France, 1924.

England, 1924.

7

Open-side Flanker

GEORGE THOMAS THOMSON (1878-1885)
Birthplace: Halifax
Position: Loose Forward
Total Caps: 9
Calcutta Cups: 2
Triple Crowns: 2
Outright Championship Victories: 2
Grand Slams: n/a
World Cups: n/a

George Thomson came into his own as rugby moved from an attritional forward-dominated game into a looser more open-attacking game.

His playing style initially confused observers and after being selected for the first ever Calcutta Cup contest in 1878 he then lost his place in the side.

Ostensibly a forward, Thomson was strong but also fast and his brilliance in the open and incessant chasing down of opponents would become more highly regarded as the game continued to evolve.

He was reselected in 1882 and was an important member of the side that, in 1883 and 1884, secured back-to-back Triple Crowns.

In all he earned nine caps and can now be regarded as the prototype loose-forward.

JOHN 'JENNY' ERIC GREENWOOD (1912-1920)
Birthplace: Lewisham
Position: Flanker
Total Caps: 13
Calcutta Cups: 3
Triple Crowns: 2
Outright Championship Victories: 2
Grand Slams: 2
World Cups: n/a

John Eric Greenwood, nicknamed 'Jenny', was first selected for England in 1912. Ostensibly a resolute tough-tackling flanker, he was equally noted for his kicking ability. His inclusion against France in 1912 helped England to a share of that year's championship. The following year he kicked points against Wales, France and Scotland on the way to securing England's first Grand Slam. This was immediately followed by a second in the final year before the outbreak of the First World War, with Greenwood landing six conversions in the final game against France.

During the war Greenwood served with the Artist's Rifles, a special forces regiment that would later become the Special Air Service regiment (SAS). He was mentioned in dispatches and wounded at Nieppe.

He suffered a further injury in the 1919 Varsity Match and had intended to retire from the game until persuaded otherwise. In 1920 the 5 Nations Championship resumed for the first time since 1914 and Greenwood, a survivor of that team, was made captain.

Greenwood's penalty and conversion ensured a narrow victory against France and further points against Ireland and Scotland gave his side a share of the Championship.

He retired at the end of the season with thirteen caps, having scored thirty points. In later life he was a director of Boots PLC and RFU President in the 1930s.

ARTHUR 'FREDDIE' FREDERICK BLAKISTON
(1920-1925)
Birthplace: West Derby
Position: Flanker
Total Caps: 17
Calcutta Cups: 4
Triple Crowns: 3
Outright Championship Victories: 3
Grand Slams: 3
World Cups: n/a

Freddie Blakiston's appearance, with his deep-set eyes, black moustache and slicked-back hair, was sometimes described as terrier-like. The way that he relentlessly tore around the field chasing down his opponents in a pack that included the likes of Wakefield, Conway and Voyce probably contributed to this image.

After receiving an MC during the First World War, Blakiston earned his first cap in the final game of the 1920 season. The following season he scored tries against Ireland and France, helping England to a Grand Slam. He starred again in the 1923 season and played in every round of the 1924 season, during which England secured a second consecutive Grand Slam. He played his final game for England in 1925, having earned seventeen caps.

Away from rugby Blakiston eventually became Sir Arthur Blakiston, 7th Baronet, and continued hunting as Master of South Shropshire Foxhounds.

WILLIAM WAVELL WAKEFIELD (1920-1927)
Birthplace: Beckenham
Position: Flanker
Total Caps: 31
Calcutta Cups: 5
Triple Crowns: 3
Outright Championship Victories: 3
Grand Slams: 3
World Cups: n/a

William Wavell Wakefield is one of the most celebrated English rugby players of all time. His total of thirty-one caps was an English record for over forty years and he was still being described as England's greatest ever forward in 1983 when he passed away at the age of eighty-five. He came to the attention of the England selectors as captain of the RAF side and when playing for Harlequins in 1919. The following year he made his debut as rugby reconvened in the aftermath of the First World War.

Wakefield settled in quickly, scoring against Ireland in Dublin, and by the end of his first season he was integral to the side and pack leader to the forwards. The following year he helped England to a Grand Slam and repeated the feat two seasons later in 1923. The natural heir to Dave Davies, he was made captain in 1924 and immediately led his side to an unprecedented third Grand Slam in four seasons.

Wakefield was a modern loose wing-forward who also spent time at No. 8 and in the second row. He was also a thinker and introduced defensive set-plays in the scrum and in the loose. In both 1923 and 1924 he led by example, scoring the opening tries in the decisive games of the series.

His ingenuity and bravery was not limited to the football field. Growing up in the Lake District he learned to fly and land aeroplanes on Lake Windermere. During the First World War he became one of the first men to successfully land a fighter biplane on an aircraft carrier (the first had perished in the act). After the war he remained with the RAF and flew as a Flight Lieutenant in the Second World War at the age of forty-one. In later life he served as a member of parliament and as president of the Rugby Football Union.

Wakefield described rugby as 'a game of beauty and power'.

REGINALD HIGGINS (1954-1959)

Birthplace: Widnes
Position: Flanker
Total Caps: 13
Calcutta Cups: 3
Triple Crowns: 1
Outright Championship Victories: 1
Grand Slams: 1
World Cups: n/a

Though his father and uncle were both Rugby League players, a career in the army meant that Reg Higgins would adopt the union code. A powerful running wing-forward, his forward drives were as difficult to stop as his defence was solid.

He was first selected for England in 1954 and his all-round game, energy and intensity won him a place in a developing England side.

The following year he would be selected for the 1955 British and Irish Lions tour of South Africa and played in a game that would later be described as the greatest of all time. The Lions won 23-22 but Higgins suffered a serious leg injury that would keep him out of the game for more than a year. In spite of the injury he instructed his stretcher bearers to wait at the side of the pitch while he watched his teammate Cliff Morgan score.

In 1957 Higgins returned to the England side in advance of what was expected to be a serious push for the championship. In those years any side that wanted to win the championship would have to deal with that man Cliff Morgan of Wales. This Higgins did magnificently in Cardiff, helping England to a narrow 3-0 victory.

Several weeks later it was Higgins' man of the match performance against Scotland, setting up one try and scoring another himself, that delivered England their first Grand Slam since 1928.

DEREK 'BUDGE' PRIOR ROGERS (1961-1969)

Birthplace: Bedford
Position: Flanker
Total Caps: 34
Calcutta Cups: 4
Triple Crowns: 0
Outright Championship Victories: 1
Grand Slams: 0
World Cups: n/a

Budge Rogers was a mainstay of the English side for nine seasons. By the time he hung up his boots he was England's most capped player, his thirty-four appearances surpassing a record that William Wavell Wakefield had held since 1927. Like Wakefield, Rogers was a chasing wing-forward who consistently stood out on account of his work-rate, commitment and ability to hunt down an opposing fly-half.

He made his debut in 1961 and kept his place in the side throughout a decade marked by inconsistent selection elsewhere. In 1963 he featured in every game of England's successful championship-winning season. He was made captain of England in 1966, and in 1969 led his side to home victories over France and Scotland.

In 1969 Budge Rogers became the first Englishman to receive an OBE for services to rugby football.

ANTHONY NEARY (1971-1980)
Birthplace: Manchester
Position: Flanker
Total Caps: 43
Calcutta Cups: 3
Triple Crowns: 1
Outright Championship Victories: 1
Grand Slams: 1
World Cups: n/a

Tony Neary is purported to have grown up playing basketball. Nonetheless he was sufficiently comfortable on a rugby field to have represented England at U15, U19 and U25 levels before touring Japan and East Asia with an England XV in 1971.

A relentless flanker, blessed with speed, stamina and game awareness, Neary would track the ball during matches so that he could be on hand to secure possession at the breakdown. He earned his first cap against Wales in 1971 and would hold down a regular place in the side for most of the remainder of the decade.

Despite the 1970s being difficult years for England, Neary's performances were consistently excellent. In 1972 he and his side secured a rare victory in South Africa. The following year he landed tries in Auckland and at Twickenham to help England to their first ever away victory against New Zealand and a home victory against Australia.

In 1980, his final season as an international, Neary, the great survivor, was ever present as England secured their first Grand Slam since 1957. His captain Bill Beaumont described him as 'the best openside I've ever played with or against'.

His total of forty-three England caps remained an English record until it was surpassed by Rory Underwood in 1991.

PETER JAMES WINTERBOTTOM (1982-1993)

Birthplace: Horsforth
Position: Flanker
Total Caps: 58
Calcutta Cups: 4 (+1 retained)
Triple Crowns: 2
Outright Championship Victories: 2
Grand Slams: 2
World Cups: Finalist

When Peter Winterbottom first broke onto the international scene during the 1981/82 season, commentators had difficulty summing up his attributes. This wasn't because his game lacked in any department but because he seemed to be able to do almost anything.

Hard-tackling, fast and often uncompromising he quickly became the scourge of England's opponents and one of the mainstays of the English side throughout the 1980s and early 1990s. He would represent England at the 1987 and 1991 Rugby World Cups, starting in the final of the latter.

The 1980s were mostly lean years for England however, and Winterbottom would have to wait to experience success with the national side. This finally came in 1991 and 1992 when he played in every round of two seasons that delivered back-to-back English Grand Slams for the first time since 1924.

Included in his fifty-eight caps were victories over all four major southern hemisphere sides.

NEIL ANTHONY BACK (1994-2003)

Birthplace: Coventry
Position: Flanker
Total Caps: 66
Calcutta Cups: 6
Triple Crowns: 3
Outright Championship Victories: 3
Grand Slams: 1
World Cups: 1

'Look Neil, it's quite simple. All you have to do is grow another 5 inches and then you can come on the plane with the other boys,' said England Team Manager Geoff Cooke when Neil Back pressed his case for inclusion in the England squad. Lesser men might have grown despondent at such words. Back could do nothing about his height so instead he put on an additional 19 lbs of muscle and pushed himself to unprecedented levels of fitness for an amateur sportsman.

'Just one cap is all I will need. I'll show the whole world what I can do then' he said after being overlooked again in 1994. Lightening quick, utterly fearless and totally committed to the contact areas, it was inevitable that he would eventually force his way in.

His call-up finally came later that year, and in 1997 he played alongside Lawrence Dallaglio and Richard Hill for the first time in what would become a legendary English back-row trio. From that point onwards Back and England were a rising force in world rugby.

He helped his side to Triple Crowns in 1998 and 2002 and outright championship victories in 2000 and 2001. In 2003, at the age of thirty-four, he was an integral member of the most successful English rugby side in history, winning a Grand Slam and the 2003 Rugby World Cup.

The World Cup final was to be the last of his sixty-six caps.

LEWIS 'MAD DOG' WALTON MOODY (2001-2011)
Birthplace: Ascot
Position: Flanker
Total Caps: 71
Calcutta Cups: 1 (+1 retained)
Triple Crowns: 2
Outright Championship Victories: 1
Grand Slams: 1
World Cups: 1

The spiritual heir to Freddie Blakiston, Lewis 'Mad Dog' Moody earned his nickname through his willingness to chase. Always the first to contest possession from restarts and often the first into the tackle area, Moody never gave his opponents an inch.

He first broke into the England team in 2001 and scored three tries in his first five caps. Despite it being a period of enormous strength in depth for the English back row he featured regularly as the team claimed a Triple Crown in 2002 and contributed a try in a win against the All-Blacks later that year.

In 2003 he helped England to a Grand Slam before making impressive contributions to the 2003 Rugby World Cup campaign and helping England into the semi-finals. In the final two rounds he featured as a super-sub and it was his stolen lineout that eventually led to Jonny Wilkinson landing the winning dropped goal in the final.

In 2007 Moody returned from injury in time to help turn around England's faltering World Cup campaign and spearhead a drive to a second consecutive final.

At the end of the 2010 season Martin Johnson selected his former teammate as captain, sparking a rejuvenation of the side's fortunes with Moody contributing to a convincing victory over Australia later that year. In 2011 Moody featured in his third consecutive World Cup, leading his side to the quarter-finals.

Moody retired with seventy-one caps, including eleven as captain, and nine tries.

8

No. 8

EDWARD TEMPLE GURDON (1878-1886)
Birthplace: Barnham Brook
Position: No. 8
Total Caps: 16
Calcutta Cups: 3 (+2 retained)
Triple Crowns: 2
Outright Championship Victories: 2
Grand Slams: n/a
World Cups: n/a

England's long tradition of commanding back-row forwards began with Edward Temple Gurdon. His energy and work-rate quickly established him in the English XV and his ability to adapt, from pushing to dribbling and latterly to passing, as the game evolved, ensured his longevity.

Gurdon was promoted to captain in 1882 in time to lead England out for the very first Home Nations Championship the following year. Under Gurdon's stewardship England won every game that year and the next, helping England become the first back-to-back winners of the Triple Crown.

At a time when international careers tended to burn bright and fast Gurdon's lasted for nine consecutive seasons. His sixteen caps remained an English record at the turn of the twentieth century. Remarkably, for a career so long, he retired with an 84 per cent win record.

JOHN 'JACK' ABBOTT KING (1911-1913)
Birthplace: Leeds
Position: No. 8
Total Caps: 12
Calcutta Cups: 2
Triple Crowns: 1
Outright Championship Victories: 1
Grand Slams: 1
World Cups: n/a

At 5 feet 5 inches Jack King is one of the shortest players to have represented England. But King didn't let his lack of stature diminish his impact on the field.

On the contrary: the closer to the ground you were, the closer you were to Jack's Kingdom. As a player he is commonly regarded as one of the finest tacklers England has produced.

King made his debut in 1911 and was an integral member of the England Grand Slam-winning side of 1913. Earning twelve caps in total he was on the winning side eight times. On one memorable occasion at Twickenham he had to be physically prevented from returning to the field after sustaining multiple broken ribs.

Like many of his teammates, King enlisted in 1914 and went to serve in France. He gave his life at the Somme in 1916 at the age of thirty-two. In his last letter home he movingly wrote 'so long as I don't disgrace the old Rugby game, I don't think I mind'.

JOHN MACGREGOR KENDALL-CARPENTER
(1949-1954)
Birthplace: Cardiff
Position: No. 8
Total Caps: 24
Calcutta Cups: 4
Triple Crowns: 1
Outright Championship Victories: 1
Grand Slams: 0
World Cups: n/a

John Carps, as he was known to his teammates, was one of the fastest back-row forwards that England ever produced. His ability to sprint across for last-ditch tackles led one opponent to say 'If you're playing against John, you've two full-backs to beat.'

Kendall-Carpenter came late to the game but was selected for Oxford in 1948. He earned his first England cap in 1949 and went on to win twenty-three including three as captain. In 1953 he was a member of the side that claimed England's first outright championship since 1937.

Away from rugby, Kendall-Carpenter was a schoolteacher and later headmaster. In 1987 he was chairman of the committee that arranged the inaugural Rugby World Cup.

ANDREW GEORGE RIPLEY (1972-1976)
Birthplace: Liverpool
Position: No. 8
Total Caps: 24
Calcutta Cups: 2
Triple Crowns: 0
Outright Championship Victories: 0
Grand Slams: 0
World Cups: n/a

Andy Ripley came from nowhere to represent England at the age of twenty-five, in only his second season with Rossyln Park. At 6 feet 5 inches it is perhaps no surprise that he caught the eye of selectors with his long strides and athleticism, unusual in a No. 8 in any era.

Having such a fast and mobile No. 8 allowed the English side of the early 1970s to surprise opponents and Ripley was put to good use in victories over South Africa in 1971 and New Zealand in 1972. In 1973 he completed a southern hemisphere clean sweep by scoring England's second try in a 20-3 home drubbing of Australia. The win crowned a season in which England had won both of their home games to earn a unique five way share of the 5 Nations championship.

Ripley earned the last of his twenty-four caps in 1976. He was a chartered accountant and became a regular contributor to rugby publications, where his quirky and irreverent wit was always well received. He continued playing for Rosslyn Park until the age of forty-one.

Ripley was diagnosed with prostate cancer in 2005 and eventually lost his life to the illness in 2010. In between he wrote a book about his struggle, the foreword to which included the following lines:

'Dare we hope? We dare. Can we hope? We can. Should we hope? We must, because to do otherwise is to waste the most precious of gifts, given so freely by God to all of us.'

JOHN PHILIP SCOTT (1978-1984)
Birthplace: Exeter
Position: No. 8
Total Caps: 34
Calcutta Cups: 3 (+1 retained)
Triple Crowns: 1
Outright Championship Victories: 1
Grand Slams: 1
World Cups: n/a

John Scott's combative style, clever work around the base of the scrum and at the tail of the lineout first brought him to the attention of England selectors in 1978. He quickly made the No. 8 position his own, although at 6 feet 4 inches and 16.5 stone he was also put to use as an auxiliary lock.

His international career peaked in 1980 when he helped England to a first Grand Slam since 1957, scoring a try in their opening win against Ireland. In 1983 he helped England to a 15-9 win against New Zealand.

Scott had considerable success as captain of Cardiff during the 1980s. He captained England four times and amassed thirty-four caps in total.

DEAN RICHARDS (1986-1996)
Birthplace: Nuneaton
Position: No. 8
Total Caps: 48
Calcutta Cups: 6 (+1 retained)
Triple Crowns: 4
Outright Championship Victories: 4
Grand Slams: 3
World Cup: Finalist

Dean Richards marked his international debut with two tries against Ireland in 1986. His all-action performances, prodigious work-rate and usefulness in the ruck and maul quickly endeared him to fans and he became a regular fixture in the English back row for more than a decade.

A forward's forward with his sleeves rolled-up and socks rolled down, Richards was occasionally accused of lacking pace. If this were true he more than made up for it with game awareness that, more often than not, allowed him to be the first to arrive at the breakdown.

His match-winning performance allowed England to defeat Australia in 1988. In 1991 he helped England reach the Rugby World Cup Final in between back-to-back Grand Slams in 1991 and 1992. He was part of the teams that defeated New Zealand and South Africa in 1993 and 1994 and added a third Grand Slam to his collection in 1995.

In 1996, his final season, he helped England to an outright championship victory and Triple Crown. In all, he amassed 48 caps.

BENJAMIN BEVAN CLARKE (1992-1999)
Birthplace: Bishop's Stortford
Position: No. 8
Total Caps: 40
Calcutta Cups: 4
Triple Crowns: 3
Outright Championship Victories: 2
Grand Slams: 1
World Cups: Semi-Finalist

As a youngster Ben Clarke once gave up rugby to concentrate on soccer. Fortunately for England he changed his mind. At 6 feet 5 inches and 17 stone he typified the type of muscular, athletic, super-athlete that would inhabit the back row in the professional age.

His speed and strength made him a natural line-breaker and while he was adept across the back row his preferred position was at No. 8.

He earned the first of his forty senior caps against South Africa in 1992. He was part of the 1995 Grand Slamming-winning side and added an outright championship victory in 1996 and Triple Crowns in 1996, 1997.

In 1996 he became the first £1 million player when transferring to Richmond FC.

MARTIN EDWARD CORRY (1997-2007)
Birthplace: Birmingham
Position: Back-row
Total Caps: 64
Calcutta Cups: 1
Triple Crowns: 1
Outright Championship Victories: 2
Grand Slams: 0
World Cups: 1

Martin Corry was a powerfully destructive ball carrier who did his best work when driving his team forward from the base of the scrum. At 6 feet 5 inches, Corry had the strength and versatility to play across the back row and in the second row and did so in an international career that began in 1997.

Substitute performances in 2000 and 2001 helped England to outright championships as England grew in stature. A Triple Crown followed in 2002 before Corry appeared in the group stages of the 2003 Rugby World Cup which England eventually won.

In 2005 Corry was installed as captain and led his side into the 2007 Rugby World Cup. After early disappointment against South Africa Corry put in a captain's performance by scoring two tries to help England to a narrow victory over Samoa. The result resurrected England's campaign and preceded a powerful charge to the final of the tournament, during which Corry was instrumental in wins against Australia and France.

The defeat in the final, against South Africa at Stade de France, was to be the last of Corry's sixty-four appearances, including seventeen as captain.

LORENZO 'LAWRENCE' BRUNO NERO DALLAGLIO (1995-2007)
Birthplace: Shepherds Bush
Position: No. 8
Total Caps: 85
Calcutta Cups: 7
Triple Crowns: 5
Outright Championship Victories: 4
Grand Slams: 1
World Cups: 1

Lawrence Dallaglio made waves as a youth before emerging as an outstanding member of England's Rugby Sevens World Cup-winning side in 1993. His lithe frame and athleticism marked him out as an open-side flanker during his early years and it was in this position that he made his England debut in 1995.

Dallaglio however had several tools at his disposal and his increasing strength, allied to his bravery and commitment at the breakdown, would see him earn caps across the back row until he eventually established himself at No. 8, in between Richard Hill and Neil Back as a key component in England's most feared and successful back-row unit.

Along with relentless commitment on the field Dallaglio possessed a charm and eloquence off it, which saw him popularly instated as England captain in 1997. He helped England to an outright championship win in 1996, his first season, and Triple Crowns in 1996, 1997 and 1998.

In 2000 England entered a prolonged period of international strength and Dallaglio added Championship wins in 2000 and 2001, a Triple Crown in 2002 and back-to-back home wins against New Zealand, Australia and South Africa.

In 2003 he added a Grand Slam and away wins against New Zealand and Australia before becoming the only member of the England squad to earn the distinction of having played in every minute of every game during England's 2003 Rugby World Cup-winning campaign.

In 2004 he returned as captain and appeared in a second consecutive World Cup Final in 2007. He earned eighty-five caps in total, twenty-two as captain.

During Dallaglio's career England became the number one team in the world. When questioned on the desire of other teams to beat them he gave an insight into the mentality of his all-conquering side by replying 'we want to beat them. A lot. All the time'.

NICHOLAS JAMES EASTER (2006-2015)*
Birthplace: Epsom
Position: No. 8
Total Caps: 51*
Calcutta Cups: 2 (+1 retained)*
Triple Crowns: 0*
Outright Championship Victories: 1*
Grand Slams: 0*
World Cups: Finalist*

Nick Easter came into the side during the 2007 6 Nations season as a late contender for a place in the squad that would seek to defend England's status as world champions during the 2007 Rugby World Cup. He solidified his place in that squad with an extraordinary demolition job against Wales during which he scored four tries and helped England to her biggest ever victory over her neighbours.

His safe hands and imposing presence in the back row quickly led to him becoming established as England's regular No. 8 and he helped carry England to a second successive Rugby World Cup final later that year.

In 2011 Easter was an integral part of a side who claimed an outright championship for the first time since 2003, and Easter became the first England captain since Martin Johnson to receive the 6 Nations trophy.

Easter looked to have completed his international career after reaching the quarter-finals of the 2011 World Cup but made an unexpected return to the side in 2015 at the age of thirty-six. His cameo helped England to a memorable victory against Wales in the Millennium Stadium and he added his sixth international try against Italy.

* At the time of writing (2015) Nick Easter is the only player included in this publication who remains a member of the England squad.

The 1957 Team

England made steady improvements in the years immediately after the Second World War and a strong group of players, led by Nim Hall and assisted by the likes of Don White and Eric Evans, delivered an outright championship in 1953. Centre Jeff Butterfield had made a try scoring debut midway through that season and his craft and endeavour would help England to a Triple Crown in 1954.

D. L. Sanders struggles against Ireland, 1954.

A disappointing year followed prompting selectors to make wholesale changes in advance of the 1956 season. Ron 'The Badger' Jacobs came into the front row. In the engine room David Marques and John Currie would become one of England's most enduring and effective second-row partnerships, adding weight and mobility to the scrum and significantly improving the English set piece. Peter Robbins and, later, Reg Higgins brought vigour to the back-row and completed a pack that would not be outmuscled.

In the backs, scrum-half Dickie Jeeps added defensive tenacity and profited from the effectiveness of the front-eight who allowed him to supply quick-ball to the likes of Butterfield and a slippery wing by the name of Peter Jackson, operating on the flank.

The choice of captain was complicated by the fact that Evans had been dropped from the 1955 side. The consensus was that he had been missed, not least for his terrier-like commitment on the field but also for the way he marshalled and motivated his players in the dressing room. Evans, at the age of thirty-four, did not take the captaincy lightly and set about fostering a sense of comradery among his team that began to bear fruit in 1957.

England v Ireland, 1958.

England were drawn away in their opening fixture against a Wales side that featured Cliff Morgan at fly-half. A game of controlled possession followed with the English back row keeping the ball away from the Welsh backs. A single penalty gave the visitors a 3-0 win and England moved on to Dublin.

A second intense display of ruthless efficiency followed with England dominant at the set-piece and her back row controlling possession. A piece of individual brilliance allowed Jackson to score the game's only try and England ran out 6-0 winners.

On a roll, Jackson employed his side-step to good effect in the following match, scoring two tries in the first-half against France. The French came back into the game in the second-half before captain Evans scored the try that would settle the match 9-6 in England's favour.

In the week leading up to England's final game against Scotland a newspaper coined the phrase 'Grand Slam' as a description for England's achievement, should they finish the season having defeated all four opponents.

Having hit on a winning formula England pursued a similar game plan at Twickenham, wearing down Scotland with forward pressure to grind out a 3-0 lead at the interval. In the second-half England cut loose with tries from Higgins and Peter Thompson and a further seven points from the boot of Robert Challis for a 16-3 victory.

Having delivered a first Grand Slam since 1928, Evans' side added an outright-Championship victory the following year.

England v Scotland match ticket, 1957.

Peter Jackson scores a try in the England v France fixture, 1957.

9

Scrum-half

CECIL 'K' ASHWORTH KERSHAW (1920-1923)
Birthplace: Dacca
Position: Scrum-half
Total Caps: 16
Calcutta Cups: 4
Triple Crowns: 2
Outright Championship Victories: 2
Grand Slams: 2
World Cups: n/a

Inset: Cecil Kershaw's England Rose.

Cecil Kershaw's other sport was fencing and it was perhaps that sport that imbued him with the speed of thought necessary to be an international scrum-half. Powerfully built he directed the scrum and was a master of the long-pass, most often to his Royal Navy and England partner Dave Davies.

The Davies-Kershaw midfield axis is the stuff of legends. Kershaw earned fourteen of his sixteen caps alongside Davies and together they never lost a game.

A perfectly executed cut through brought a try against Scotland during his debut season of 1920 and he followed that up with another against Wales at the start of the 1921 season. A Grand Slam was secured that year and another in 1923.

Kershaw didn't lose a single game against Scotland, Ireland or France and retired from international rugby with an 84 per cent win percentage record.

ARTHUR TUDOR YOUNG (1924-1929)
Birthplace: Darjeeling
Position: Scrum-half
Total Caps: 19
Calcutta Cups: 2
Triple Crowns: 2
Outright Championship Victories: 2
Grand Slams: 2
World Cups: n/a

Known as the 'Little Man', at 5 feet 5 inches Arthur Young was the archetypal diminutive scrum-half. One opponent commented 'Whenever we kicked a blade of grass, there was Arthur Young behind it.'

Since the days of Dai Gent the accepted role of the scrum-half had been to feed the backs from the base of the scrum; Arthur Young had other ideas. A master of the feint and duck, he perfected the art of 'slithering' or dodging past flankers.

His approach brought immediate dividends as England secured a Grand Slam in Young's first international season of 1924. He featured in the side regularly over the next five seasons and in 1928 played in every game of a season in which England defeated Australia and secured another Grand Slam.

In total Young amassed nineteen caps. Away from rugby he was a soldier in the British Indian Army and died on active service in 1933, aged thirty-one.

BERNARD CECIL GADNEY (1932-1938)
Birthplace: Oxford
Position: Scrum-half
Total Caps: 14
Calcutta Cups: 4
Triple Crowns: 2
Outright Championship Victories: 2
Grand Slams: n/a
World Cups: n/a

Bernard Gadney was one of a new breed of strong, tall scrum-halfs who had broken through in response to the spoiling tactics of opposition wing-forwards. He was also unusually athletic. To aid his fitness regime he would regularly get off the train at nearby Richmond on international days and run the rest of the way to the stadium with his kit-bag.

His height afforded him several weapons on the field, not the least of which was a fast, accurate pass that allowed him to spray balls out from the base of the scrum directly to the wing. This facilitated a useful partnership with Prince Alexander Obolensky and the two became friends as well as teammates.

He was first selected for England in 1932 and instated as captain at the start of the 1934 season. That same season Gadney led England to a first Triple Crown since 1928. In 1936 Gadney became the first English captain to lead his side to victory over New Zealand.

Gadney remained in and around the side until 1938 and played a part in a second Triple Crown-winning season in 1937. He earned fourteen caps in all, eight as captain.

RICHARD 'DICKIE' ERIC GAUTREY JEEPS (1956-1962)
Birthplace: Willingham
Position: Scrum-half
Total Caps: 24
Calcutta Cups: 3 (+2 retained)
Triple Crowns: 2
Outright Championship Victories: 2
Grand Slams: 1
World Cups: n/a

As a schoolboy Dickie Jeeps was a full-back, but at the age of fifteen he made the transition to scrum-half. There he developed into one of England's best defensive halves, tackling with relish and stubbornly refusing to part with the ball unless to set-up the attacking breaks of his fly-half.

In 1955 Jeeps was called up to partner Cliff Morgan in the successful 1955 British and Irish Lions tour of South Africa. As one of the Lions standout performers he was selected for England the following year. His debut however didn't go according to plan. England were defeated by Wales and Jeeps was dropped. But the following year he played in every game and in doing so helped England to their first Grand Slam since 1928. Jeeps and England retained the Championship in 1958, and in 1960 the scrum-half captained his side to a Triple Crown.

In all Jeeps earned twenty-four caps, thirteen as captain, and was selected for three consecutive Lions tours. Away from rugby he was a fruit farmer and served as president of the Rugby Football Union in 1976-77.

STEVE JAMES SMITH (1973-1983)
Birthplace: Stockport
Position: Scrum-half
Total Caps: 28
Calcutta Cups: 3 (+ 1 retained)
Triple Crowns: 1
Outright Championship Victories: 1
Grand Slams: 1
World Cups: n/a

Steve Smith had the ominous task of replacing Bill Beaumont as England captain in 1982. For the selectors Smith was an obvious choice as for several years the lively scrum-half had commanded one of the most feared packs in world rugby.

Smith made his debut in 1973 during a unique season in which a five-way split of the Championship occurred. England shared in this by winning both of their home games and later that year added Australia to their list of Twickenham scalps.

Smith's next notable success with the national side came in the 1980 Grand Slam-winning campaign. Smith played his part in this most notably by putting in a match-winning, try-scoring performance against Ireland in the opening fixture. He would score another sensational try against Scotland in the deciding fixture.

In all Smith earned twenty-eight caps, five as captain – an honour which he described as 'the ultimate accolade'.

NIGEL DAVID MELVILLE (1984-1988)
Birthplace: Leeds
Position: Scrum-half
Total Caps: 13
Calcutta Cups: 1
Triple Crowns: 0
Outright Championship Victories: 0
Grand Slams: 0
World Cups: 0

Only a handful of English players were held in such high esteem by selectors that they were given the England captaincy on their debut. Nigel Melville was one of them, leading England out against Australia at the age of just twenty-three.

'The essential skill of the scrum-half is the pass' said Melville and it was his quick hands and ability to pass short, long and in either direction that quickly earned him praise.

He captained England seven times and made thirteen appearances in total. In his final cap he suffered a serious injury during a game in which England were trailing Ireland. When his teammates voiced their concern Melville gave them one simple instruction: 'say it with tries'.

The team returned to the field and notched up six unanswered second-half tries in his honour.

Melville remained in the game after retiring and guided Wasps and Gloucester to league and cup success before becoming President of Operations for USA Rugby.

RICHARD JOHN HILL (1984-1991)
Birthplace: Birmingham
Position: Scrum-half
Total Caps: 29
Calcutta Cups: 1
Triple Crowns: 1
Outright Championship Victories: 1
Grand Slams: 1
World Cups: Finalist

Richard Hill developed a reputation for being 'hot-headed' early in his career. But it was this fiery determination, as much as his quick pass, that lead to his international call-up in 1984, and by 1987 he was deemed sufficiently calm to be given the captaincy.

As captain he liked to instil confidence in his players and lead by example by giving 100 per cent effort. In preparing for the 1987 Rugby World Cup he cited 'mental attitude, the will to win and pride when you put on the England jersey' as essential qualities.

These qualities he retained when embarking on an unbroken run of twenty appearances, a run that culminated, in 1991, with England's first Grand Slam in eleven seasons and an inspired charge to the final of the 1991 Rugby World Cup.

The scrum-half ended his career at the top, having earned twenty-nine caps, including three as captain.

COLIN DEWI MORRIS (1988-1995)
Birthplace: Crickhowell
Position: Scrum-half
Total Caps: 26
Calcutta Cups: 3 (+1 retained)
Triple Crowns: 2
Outright Championship Victories: 2
Grand Slams: 2
World Cups: Semi-finalist

Gareth Chilcott maintains that Morris may have decided to become a rugby player after being flattened by a herd of stampeding bulls as a young boy.

The first thing that most people noticed about him wasn't his dive-pass but his name. Morris isn't the first Welshman to play for England but the situation did bring about some consternation in the early days. His club teammates chose to call him Derek. When asked why he chose to represent England he replied 'England gave me a chance to realise a dream'.

What he brought to his adopted homeland however was an unpredictable streak from outside the scrum. Morris was powerfully built for a scrum-half and had the strength to break through opponents. He would also vary his game depending on which of his forwards or backs he thought most likely to win the game.

He scored a try in beating Australia on his debut and landed two more during England's 1992 Grand Slam season. He helped England to wins against South Africa and New Zealand before helping England to fourth place in the 1995 Rugby World Cup.

He earned twenty-six caps in total.

KYRAN PAUL PATRICK BRACKEN (1993-2003)
Birthplace: Dublin
Position: Scrum-Half
Total Caps: 51
Calcutta Cups: 5
Triple Crowns: 4
Outright Championship Victories: 3
Grand Slams: 2
World Cups: 1

Kyran Bracken had his ankle deliberately stamped on within minutes of his international debut against New Zealand in 1993. But Bracken played on with admirable resolve and helped earn his side a first victory over the All-Blacks in more than a decade.

A scrum-half with excellent vision, Bracken had the ability to turn defence quickly into attack and brought skill and aggression to the sides in which he played. By 1995 he had established himself as England's first choice scrum-half and played in every round of a 5 Nations campaign that secured a Grand Slam.

Triple Crowns were added in 1998 and 2002 and substitute appearances helped England to another outright championship in 2001, a year in which he captained the side three times in North America.

In 2003 Bracken was a member of the England squad that delivered the most successful calendar year in English rugby history, adding another Grand Slam and Rugby World Cup to his list of accolades.

He earned the last of his fifty-one caps during the tournament.

MATTHEW JAMES SUTHERLAND DAWSON (1995-2006)
Birthplace: Birkenhead
Position: Scrum-Half
Total Caps: 77
Calcutta Cups: 7
Triple Crowns: 4
Outright Championship Victories: 4
Grand Slams: 1
World Cups: 1

Matt Dawson broke into the national squad at a time when England had considerable strength in depth, particularly at scrum-half. For large parts of his career Dawson would jostle with the likes of Kyran Bracken and Austin Healey for his place.

But Dawson was a fierce competitor whose confidence, grit, speed and impudence normally won through. His quick hands and tackling ability, allied to a positive and aggressive mindset, helped England to an outright championship and Triple Crown in his first full season, in 1996.

Dawson starred in the 1997 British and Irish Lions tour of South Africa before scoring two tries to help England win another Triple Crown in 1998. The following year he captained the national side on a gruelling tour of the southern hemisphere and in 2000 he captained England to two wins that would deliver an outright championship.

From 2000 onwards Dawson was part of a core of players around whom England's most successful side was built. He contributed tries on the way to outright championships in 2000 and 2001 and consecutive wins over the three southern-hemisphere sides in 2002.

In 2003 he helped England to a Grand Slam before the 2003 Rugby World Cup, during which he set up Jonny Wilkinson's drop-kick in the final that would deliver his side the Webb Ellis Cup for the first time.

He continued to represent England until 2006 and earned seventy-seven caps in total.

10

Fly-half

ALAN ROTHERHAM (1882-1887)
Birthplace: Coventry
Position: Half-back
Total Caps: 12
Calcutta Cups: 2 (+2 retained)
Triple Crowns: 2
Outright Championship Victories: 2
Grand Slams: n/a
World Cups: n/a

It is now universally accepted that one of the primary functions of the fly-half is to link the forwards with the backs, but it was not always this way. It was the sharp mind of Alan Rotherham that first introduced what was initially described as 'Rotherham's Game' by way of his mixture of passing and darting runs.

Once Rotherham had brought about this change the fast, creative, attacking aspects of the game came into being and brought immediate dividends to the England side. He made a wining debut against Wales in 1882. The following season he helped England to the first ever Triple Crown before repeating the trick when playing in every round of the 1884 season.

In total he earned twelve caps and lost only once.

JAMES 'DARKIE' PETERS (1906-1908)
Birthplace: Salford
Position: Fly-half
Total Caps: 5
Calcutta Cups: 1
Triple Crowns: 0
Outright Championship Victories: 0
Grand Slams: n/a
World Cups: n/a

Jimmy Peters is England's first black international rugby player and his story is one of personal tragedy, discrimination and salvation through rugby.

Born in Salford to an English mother and West-Indian father, both he and his father were circus performers. While Jimmy was a bareback horse rider, his father was a lion tamer and lost his life when mauled by one of the animals when Jimmy was still a boy.

At the age of eleven Jimmy sustained a broken arm and the circus, being unable to support him, left him with an orphanage close to Blackheath, where Jimmy would visit and watch the celebrated local rugby team.

After training as a carpenter Peters played rugby in Bristol and Plymouth where he developed into an elusive running fly-half with accurate place-kicking and a knack of feinting his way out of tackles.

He was selected to play at county level for Devon, and in 1906 received a call-up from the RFU at a time when the England side was in perpetual struggle. On his debut Jimmy helped England win the Calcutta Cup for the first time in four seasons. In his next match he scored a try at the Parc des Princes, helping England rack up nine tries against the French.

In keeping with the times, and in spite of his evident skill, Peters would sadly encounter racism at various times during his career. In an infamous incident, when representing Devon against the 1906 touring South Africa side, the visiting Springboks refused to play against him and demanded that he be removed from the team.

The Devon side stood by their teammate and made clear that if Peters didn't play then neither did they. In the end it took an intervention from the South African commissioner to ensure that the game would go ahead and that Peters would take to the field. On receiving the command the Springbok captain is purported to have said 'well alright but we shall kill him'. Peters' captain replied 'that's alright we've been trying to for years'.

ADRIAN DURA STOOP (1905-1912)
Birthplace: Kensington
Position: Fly-half
Total Caps: 15
Calcutta Cups: 3
Triple Crowns: 1
Outright Championship Victories: 1
Grand Slams: 0
World Cups: n/a

Adrian Stoop made history when he became the first man to lead England out at Twickenham in 1910. The previous year he had led Harlequins out for the stadium's inaugural fixture.

The 1909/10 season represented the culmination of a long walk to redemption for Stoop, who had been first capped for England in 1905.

Stoop amassed five caps during lean years for England before being dropped after a rout at the hands of the Welsh during the 1907 season. Rather than lick his wounds Stoop responded to the setback with characteristic alacrity. At the time a clear division between the roles of fly-half and scrum-half were beginning to develop, but England had so far been slow to respond. The success of Harlequins and 'Stoop's system' saw him reinstated as captain at the start of the 1910 season.

His return coincided with the very first international game to be played at England's new home in Twickenham. Stoop's unpredictable style initiated a move that enabled England to land Twickenham's first international try inside the opening minute of the opening game against Wales. The score put England on course for a first victory against the Welsh since 1898 and, later that year, a first outright championship victory since 1892.

Stoop continued to play for Harlequins until 1939, retiring at the age of fifty-six. He received fifteen international caps in all and will always be remembered as the man who led England out of the post-1895 wilderness.

WILLIAM 'DAVE' JOHN ABBOTT DAVIES (1913-1923)
Birthplace: Pembroke
Position: Fly-half
Total Caps: 22
Calcutta Cups: 6
Triple Crowns: 4
Outright Championship Victories: 4
Grand Slams: 4
World Cups: n/a

W. J. A. 'Dave' Davies made his first start for England 1913 and quickly became one of the iconic players of his era. The archetypal inventive, quick-thinking fly-half, Davies was the complete rugby player whose acceleration, chips and ranged passing could turn defence into attack in an instant.

His international career lasted for eleven years and he was often the spark to whom England looked for inspiration. When his side were under pressure, his intelligent kicking came to the rescue; when they needed points he would score.

Although Davies lost his first international, incredibly he would not lose another game in an England jersey. His eleven-year spell, either side of the First World War, was a golden era of English rugby and included two of England's finest ever sides. Davies was integral to both.

His long pass to Vincent Coates allowed England to score first in Cardiff and from then on the class of 1913 didn't look back. They ran in victories against Wales, France and Scotland without conceding a point and landed four unanswered tries against Ireland in Dublin. Davies' first season had coincided with England's first Grand Slam.

The following year England did it again. In the final game against France, Davies orchestrated a nine-try drubbing, landing his first international try in the process.

He spent the duration of the First World War at sea, seeing action at the Battle of Jutland and receiving an OBE on his return in 1919.

He returned to Twickenham as captain of the Royal Navy side and was made captain of the national side in 1921. From 1920 onwards he formed one half of England's most successful ever half-back combination with scrum-half Cecil Kershaw. Davies and Kershaw would play together fourteen times without defeat.

In his first season as England captain he led his side to another Grand Slam. In 1923, his final season, he delivered an unprecedented fourth Slam, ending his international career in Paris by landing a dropped-goal in the final play of the game. His teammate, and the man who would replace him as captain, William Wavell Wakefield, was adamant that Davies had deliberately engineered the show-stopping finish.

The Welsh said that 'when Davies plays, England win' and they were right: in twenty-two games he won twenty-one times and all of his eleven games as captain. He retired with a 95 per cent win record and was England's most capped fly-half for more than sixty years.

NORMAN 'NIM' MACLEOD HALL (1947-1955)
Birthplace: Huddersfield
Position: Fly-half
Total Caps: 17
Calcutta Cups: 3
Triple Crowns: 0
Outright Championship Victories: 1
Grand Slams: 0
World Cups: n/a

Nim Hall was England's 'shining light' in the immediate post-Second World War period. A versatile fly-half, he represented England against Scotland during the 1946 Victory Internationals, before securing his first full cap the following year.

Between 1947 and 1955 he represented England on seventeen occasions – thirteen times as captain. In 1953, after having been switched to full-back, he led England to their first outright championship since 1937.

During his international career he landed eight conversions, four penalties and three dropped goals spurring Welsh centre Bleddyn Williams to comment,

'Every Welshman has reason to remember the name Nim Hall, the man who dropped more goals against Wales than the R.A.F. dropped bombs on Berlin.'

AUGUSTUS 'BEV' BEVERLEY WALTER RISMAN (1959-1961)
Birthplace: Salford
Position: Fly-half
Total Caps: 8
Calcutta Cups: 0 (+1 retained)
Triple Crowns: 0
Outright Championship Victories: 0
Grand Slams: 0
World Cups: n/a

For fans of English rugby Bev Risman will always remain a case of what might have been. A complete footballer whose vision and game-management skills might have benefitted the side for a decade was instead lost to the rival code after only a couple of seasons.

Risman can be forgiven for this however. His father, Gus Risman, is Rugby League royalty and it was only natural that his son should one day seek to emulate his feats. Bev's inclusion in this book however is down to him having made his mark on the amateur code by the time he signed professional terms.

Risman was first selected in 1959 and made an immediate impact by scoring a disallowed try within the first five minutes of his debut at Cardiff Arms Park. His exploits in his first season earned him a call-up to the 1959 British and Irish Lions with whom his try scoring and creativity helped his side to victories over Australia and New Zealand.

Sadly he never got the opportunity to make as significant an impact with England, earning just four more caps before making the switch to Rugby League.

Years later his reply, when asked to describe the mentality of the national side, would be inscribed on the walls of the Twickenham dressing room.

'Together, we would just refuse to take a backwards step.'

RICHARD ADRIAN WILLIAM SHARP (1960-1967)
Birthplace: Mysore
Position: Fly-half
Total Caps: 14
Calcutta Cups: 2
Triple Crowns: 1
Outright Championship Victories: 1
Grand Slams: 0
World Cups: n/a

Richard Sharp is one of the few men to have a game named after him. Sharp's game was the deciding fixture of the 1963 season. England went into the fixture after defeating both France and Wales and having drawn 0-0 with Ireland and knowing that victory would give them their first Championship victory since 1958. Scotland however were no pushovers and knew that a win for them would bring them their first Championship since 1938.

Cornishman Sharp had established himself in the side during the 1960 season when his mixture of incisive running and intelligent kicking had contributed to an undefeated season and share of the Championship. In 1963 he was given captaincy of the side and contributed two conversions and a dropped goal in a win against Wales in Cardiff.

But Sharp's saved his most memorable contribution until the final game of the season. England began the second-half trailing 5-8 when the fly-half embarked on a 40-yard run that flat-footed three defenders allowing him to touch down for one of the most spectacular tries in English rugby history. Subsequently converted the try was enough to give England a narrow lead, which they held until the final whistle.

He returned to the side in 1967 and earned the last of his sixteen caps when captaining the side against Australia.

Sharp is thought to have been the inspiration behind Bernard Cornwell's fictional character 'Richard Sharpe'.

CHRISTOPHER ROBERT ANDREW (1985-1997)
Birthplace: Richmond
Position: Fly-half
Total Caps: 71
Calcutta Cups: 6 (+1 retained)
Triple Crowns: 4
Outright Championship Victories: 3
Grand Slams: 3
World Cups: Finalist

Rob Andrew made his international debut in 1985 and brought immediate solidity to the spine of the England team. He was given the nickname 'Squeaky' but Andrew had teeth too, which he demonstrated by landing two dropped goals and four penalties on his debut.

During an international career that lasted more than ten years, one of England's finest sides emerged around Andrew, transforming England from perennial underachievers into a side that would establish a northern-hemisphere, English hegemony not seen since the 1920s.

Andrew's first international honours arrived in 1991 with a Grand Slam. Later the same year a late dropped goal against Scotland at Murrayfield earned England a place in the Rugby World Cup Final. Disappointment in the final was followed by a second successive Grand Slam in 1992.

In 1995 Andrew secured a third Grand Slam and yet another dramatic dropped goal gave England a World Cup quarter-final victory against Australia.

In all Andrew earned seventy-one caps, including two as captain. He amassed a then-English record of 396 points and twenty dropped goals.

Since hanging up his boots Andrew has served the game as an administrator, firstly as a director at Newcastle Falcons and latterly as a director of the Rugby Football Union.

PAUL 'LARRY' JAMES GRAYSON
(1995-2004)
Birthplace: Chorley
Position: Fly-half
Total Caps: 32
Calcutta Cups: 4
Triple Crowns: 4
Outright Championship Victories: 2
Grand Slams: 1
World Cups: 1

Paul Grayson was a semi-professional footballer for Accrington Stanley and didn't even pick up an oval ball until the age of eighteen, whereupon he discovered that he had a natural aptitude for understanding what made a side tick.

Solid technique allied to mental resilience made Grayson a reliable place kicker. When questioned on his kicking he replied, 'I don't think about missing. It doesn't enter my head. I am there to score the goal and make the points.'

He marked his debut by landing seventeen points from the boot in a win against Samoa at the tail end of 1995. The following year he helped England to outright championship success, including a Triple Crown which was retained in 1997 and 1998.

In 1999 he and his side reached the quarter-finals of the 1999 Rugby World Cup. A four-year absence from the side followed before Grayson's club form saw him return to the side in 2003. After helping England to a Grand Slam he then featured in the group stages of the 2003 Rugby World Cup, which England eventually won.

He made his final international appearance in 2004 having amassed thirty-two caps. His 400 points are second only to Jonny Wilkinson in the list of all-time England points scorers.

JONATHAN PETER WILKINSON
(1998-2011)
Birthplace: Frimley
Position: Fly-half
Total Caps: 91
Calcutta Cups: 6
Triple Crowns: 5
Outright Championship Victories: 4
Grand Slams: 1
World Cups: 1

Jonny Wilkinson was born in Frimley and became a professional rugby player with Newcastle Falcons in 1997. His ability was noted at an early age and he made his full England debut during an horrific 0-76 defeat at the hands of Australia in 1998.

Shortly afterwards Wilkinson's inventive, attacking style and metronomic consistency with the boot had earned him a spot as England's regular fly-half. In 2002 Wilkinson embarked on a run of form that elevated him among the finest rugby players in the world.

In November of that year he helped England to consecutive home victories against New Zealand, Australia and South Africa. Against the All-Blacks he was the star of the show, scoring one of Twickenham's most memorable tries as he chipped and pirouetted around a line of wrong-footed defenders.

He shone in every round of the 2003 6 Nations Championship, in particular against Ireland, when scoring one try and setting up another.

The world was now on high alert about the skills of the English fly-half but none could stop his England side in their ceaseless march to the 2003 World Cup Final in Sydney.

In the final minute of extra time, with the scores tied at 17-17, the hopes of a nation lay in the boot of the talismanic Wilkinson. He didn't let us down, landing the dropped goal that brought the Webb Ellis Cup to England and the northern hemisphere for the first time.

In 2007 Wilkinson played in a second consecutive World Cup Final, by which time he had altered his game to become the best defensive fly-half in the world. When he played his final game for England in 2011, he had mustered ninety-one caps and a record 1,179 points for his country.

Off the field Wilkinson's obsessive dedication to practice, along with his personal grace and demeanour, have elevated him to the status of a true rugby ambassador and role model for young people across the world. He was awarded the BBC's Sports Personality of the Year Award in 2003.

The 1980 Team

Fran Cotton made his debut for England in 1971, scrumming down alongside John Pullin. Tenacious flanker Tony Neary made his debut the same season and would be joined in the pack by Roger Uttley and Bill Beaumont as the decade progressed. Foot soldiers such as these meant that England would never be an easy touch but throughout the 1970s they were never quite able to threaten the stranglehold that the dominant Welsh and French held over the 5 Nations Championship.

By the end of the decade these seasoned veterans were tired of being on the outside looking in and Beaumont, whose heroic commitment as a player had seen him instated as captain in 1978, hit upon the solution.

South Stand corporate box, 1980.

Graham Mourie's touring New Zealand side arrived in Otley unbeaten in November 1979. There a side selected to represent the Northern Division and captained by Beaumont ran them ragged. After inflicting a 21-9 defeat on the All-Blacks, Beaumont went on record with a prediction that England would not only win the 1980 Championship but would claim England's first Triple Crown since 1960.

Unsurprisingly the Northern Division would supply much of the ammunition. Wing John Carleton found himself promoted to the England side at once. Cotton returned to the side, after an extended absence, to scrum down alongside Peter Wheeler and Phil Blakeway in a formidable front row that has perhaps never been bettered.

Uttley too was reselected to play alongside John Scott and the evergreen Neary in an unyielding back row. Finally Steve Smith and Dusty Hare were given extended runs in the side for the first time since making their debuts in 1973 and 1974 respectively. The class of 1980 was therefore a new-look side that was conversely stuffed full of experience.

The campaign opened at Twickenham against a strong Irish side. Constant pressure from the English pack and dominance at the set piece earned England a lead at the interval. In the second-half Tony Bond suffered a broken leg and was replaced by a livewire centre called Clive Woodward. By the end of the match England had scored three unanswered tries and Hare's boot had contributed twelve points to give England an emphatic 24-9 victory.

For their next match England travelled to Paris where they hadn't won since 1964. Once more the English forwards turned the screw in an effort to negate the skilful French backs. Despite conceding an early try the plan worked and England slowly but surely built up a ten-point lead. Wave after wave of French attack was repelled in the closing stages of the match and England held on for a 17-13 victory.

England's next game was against reigning champions Wales. Both sides were unbeaten and the game was billed as a decider though few, even among the English fans, really believed that they could win. The Welsh had just completed their most successful ever decade in rugby, having won four out of the last five championships.

The tension in the Twickenham stands was equally manifest on the pitch and things began to bubble over when Welshman Paul Ringer was sent off in the fifteenth minute. England however remained disciplined and Hare kicked his side into a three-point lead. Incensed, the Welsh replied with a try that gave them a slender half-time lead.

With the scores so close the tension increased but another Hare penalty deep into the

England v Wales match programme, 1980.

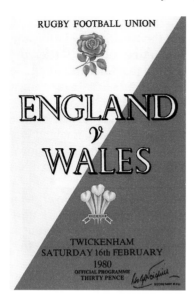

England v Wales match programme, 1980.

second-half saw the lead swap hands for a third time. With just three minutes, remaining Wales landed a second try that most thought would settle things in their favour.

Beaumont's side however were not done. Deep into injury time the referee blew for a penalty to England. With the atmosphere now so tense you could cut it with a knife, Hare showed masterly self-control to step up and calmly kick his third penalty. At 9-8. England had won.

All that now stood between England and the realisation of their captain's prophecy was Scotland at Murrayfield. What followed was England's most complete performance for many years. Once more the English scrum dominated, setting up possession for the backs, which the brilliant Woodward ruthlessly exploited. His quick ball cut the Scottish defence open, allowing Mike Slemen to open the scoring. By the end of the match Carleton had a hat-trick of tries and England a 30-18 victory.

At long last a generation of English rugby players had found the right combination to win and, as their captain had said that they would, they had done so in style.

England team, 1980.

11

Left-wing

EDGAR ROBERTS MOBBS (1909-1910)
Birthplace: Northampton
Position: Wing
Total Caps: 7
Calcutta Cups: 0
Triple Crowns: 0
Outright Championship Victories: 1
Grand Slams: 0
World Cups: n/a

Edgar Mobbs never made his school XV. But Mobbs wasn't the type of character to take no for an answer. He stuck at it and developed into a prolific try-scoring back whose unorthodox loose-limbed high-speed running, allied to a fierce hand-off, made him an extremely difficult opponent. He was selected for his country in 1909.

He scored a try against Australia on his debut and added three more during the course of the season. In 1910 he starred in England's first Championship-winning season since 1892. He was given the captaincy at Parc de Princes in a game that England won 11-3.

Mobbs was refused commission when the First World War began in 1914 due to his age – he was 32. With typical zeal he forced his way in by arranging his own fighting force – 'D Company' of the 7th Northants.

By 1916, Mobbs had risen to Lieutenant Colonel. He was killed in action the following year at the third battle of Ypres.

After the war ended a charity match between East Midlands and the Barbarians was held at Franklin Gardens in 1921. Now called the Mobbs Memorial Match, the event continues to this day.

DOUGLAS 'DAN'L' LAMBERT (1907-1911)
Birthplace: South Norwood
Position: Wing
Total Caps: 7
Calcutta Cups: 0
Triple Crowns: 0
Outright Championship Victories: 0
Grand Slams: 0
World Cups: n/a

Douglas Lambert was known to all as Dan'l. His straight-line speed and unfailing ability to receive a pass brought him several unique accolades during an England career that included seven caps. The first came in his 1907 debut when he scored an unprecedented five tries against France. Five tries on an international debut has never been equalled; five tries in an international Test-match remained a record until 1995.

Lambert was in and out of the side over the following four seasons but in 1911, again against France, he broke another record. Two tries, two penalties and five conversions earned him twenty-two points, a tally that remained unsurpassed until 1990.

He fought and eventually died at the Battle of Loos, serving with the 6th Battalion of Royal East Kent Regiment in 1915 at the age of thirty-two.

ALASTAIR MCNAUGHTON SMALLWOOD (1920-1925)
Birthplace: Alloa
Position: Wing
Total Caps: 14
Calcutta Cups: 3
Triple Crowns: 2
Outright Championship Victories: 2
Grand Slams: 2
World Cups: n/a

Alastair Smallwood was one of the great characters of 1920s rugby. After serving with the Northumberland Fusiliers during the First World War he received his first call-up to the national side in 1920 as international rugby reconvened for the first time since 1914.

An exponent of running rugby, he was originally selected among the centres, before earning the rest of his caps on the wing. He had several tricks at his disposal including a swerving run, hand-off and the ability to land long-range dropped goals. He was also a master of the bluff and on at least one occasion pretended to hand the ball back to opposition players only to accelerate past them once they were back in range.

His teammate William Wavell Wakefield described Smallwood as enterprising and clever and credited him with having introduced short lineouts to his side's attacking repertoire.

His two second-half tries against Wales in 1921 set England on their way to a Triple Crown and Grand Slam. In 1923 he scored a memorable dropped goal from close to the halfway line against Wales, before registering tries against Ireland and Scotland, to set England on their way to a second Grand Slam in three seasons.

By 1924 Smallwood had earned twelve caps and finished on the winning team in every single one of them. Born in Alloa, Scotland, it was perhaps appropriate that he earned the last of his fourteen caps during the first international to be held at Murrayfield in 1925. It would be the only time in his international career that he would taste defeat. He retired with an 86 per cent win record. Away from rugby he was a teacher.

HARRY 'HAL' SEDGEWICK SEVER (1936-1938)
Birthplace: Lavendon
Position: Wing
Total Caps: 10
Calcutta Cups: 2
Triple Crowns: 1
Outright Championship Victories: 1
Grand Slams: n/a
World Cups: n/a

Despite scoring a try on his debut to help England to their first ever victory against New Zealand in 1936, Hal Sever was completely overlooked due of the exploits of the player on the other wing who scored two! However while Prince Alexander Obolensky's England career undoubtedly peaked in that first game, Sever went on to make a more lasting impression.

His direct running and rapid acceleration created a try against Ireland later that year and he began the following season with a dropped goal to give England a 4-3 victory against Wales. A tight affair against Ireland was then settled in the dying minutes when Sever set off on an 80-yard run that saw him touch down, with a player hanging off his back, to give England a 9-8 victory.

A clean sweep and Triple Crown was secured and Sever completed a magnificent season with another try at Murrayfield. England had wrapped up the Championship with Sever contributing ten out of nineteen points in total.

Sever earned his final cap in 1938 having scored five tries in ten appearances.

DAVID JOHN DUCKHAM (1969-1976)
Birthplace: Coventry
Position: Wing
Total Caps: 36
Calcutta Cups: 2
Triple Crowns: 0
Outright Championship Victories: 0
Grand Slams: 0
World Cups: n/a

In an era of Welsh dominance David Duckham was the flag bearer for English rugby. His stealthy running, elusive swerve and side-step gave the English back-line teeth in the early 1970s.

He made his try-scoring debut against Ireland in 1969 as a centre, a position in which he would remain until he was shifted onto the wing, where he earned the majority of his thirty-six caps.

At the end of the 1969 season he helped England to a first ever victory against South Africa. In 1973 his England side earned a share of the Championship and later that year he helped England to their first ever away victory against the All-Blacks.

He also gained victories over the All-Blacks as a British and Irish Lion in 1971 and Barbarian in 1973, which led his mostly Welsh teammates giving him the nickname 'Dai'.

MIKE ANTHONY CHARLES SLEMEN (1976-1984)
Birthplace: Liverpool
Position: Wing
Total Caps: 31
Calcutta Cups: 4 (+2 retained)
Triple Crowns: 1
Outright Championship Victories: 1
Grand Slams: 1
World Cups: n/a

Mike Slemen probably saw more of the ball in his youth, as a scrum-half, and it was perhaps this that caused him to hare around the field so much, after switching to the wing at the age of twenty. His keenness and energy soon saw him progress and he made his England debut in 1976.

He was a mainstay of the England side for the following six seasons and it was he that finished off an exquisite move by Woodward to set England on the path to victory against Scotland in the ultimate game of the 1980 Grand Slam-winning season.

A measure of the affection and esteem Slemen was held in by his teammates and England fans alike can be taken by their reaction to his being knocked unconscious in a game against Australia in 1982. He was given a standing ovation as he was removed from the field and an inspired England came from behind to beat the Wallabies 15-11.

Slemen helped England to victory against New Zealand in 1983 before ending his international career with thirty-one caps and eight tries.

CHRISTOPHER OTI (1988-1991)

Birthplace: Paddington
Position: Wing
Total Caps: 13
Calcutta Cups: 1 (+1 retained)
Triple Crowns: 0
Outright Championship Victories: 0
Grand Slams: 0
World Cups: 0

Like Alexander Obolensky and Richard Sharp, Chris Oti has a game named after him. His moment in the sun came against Ireland in 1988. At the time England were assembling a new side that would go on to claim a series of major honours. In 1988 the back-line was not quite settled and Oti was among those staking a claim for the left-wing berth.

Trailing 0-3 at half-time in something of a lacklustre encounter England, and Oti in particular, stormed out of the blocks in the second-half, scoring six unanswered tries. Oti, by way of explosive pace and mesmerising footwork, landed three of them. The resultant 35-3 victory kick-started a new era in English rugby as 'Swing Low Sweet Chariot' rang around the stadium for the first time.

Oti went on to play his part in helping England to the 1991 Rugby World Cup Final and retired having scored eight tries in thirteen appearances.

RORY UNDERWOOD (1984-1996)

Birthplace: Middlesborough
Position: Wing
Total Caps: 85
Calcutta Cups: 9 (+1 retained)
Triple Crowns: 4
Outright Championship Victories: 4
Grand Slams: 3
World Cup: Finalist

Rory Underwood made his international debut in 1984 at the age of twenty. His rise to the top of English rugby was so rapid that he confessed that he still had 99 per cent of the game left to learn at a time when he had already established himself as an England regular.

Such swiftness was to be expected of Underwood. Speed and the mastery of speed were the tools that defined him, either as a lightning-fast wing, or as a fighter pilot for the Royal Air Force. His anticipation and ability to be running at top speed within moments of receiving the ball made him one of the most potent attacking players in world rugby.

His five tries against Fiji in 1989 allowed him to equal Cyril Lowe's English record of eighteen that had stood for sixty-six years. Over the next four seasons he doubled this tally, helping England to back-to-back Grand Slams and a World Cup Final in the process.

In 1995 he added a third Grand Slam before adding another outright championship victory in 1996. He retired having amassed eighty-five caps, a record for an English wing. His forty-nine international tries are also an English record.

DAN LUGER (1998-2003)
Birthplace: Chiswick
Position: Wing
Total Caps: 38
Calcutta Cups: 2
Triple Crowns: 2
Outright Championship Victories: 2
Grand Slams: 1
World Cup: 1

With a Croatian father and Czech mother, Dan Luger had options when it came to international rugby. However there was never any doubt who he would eventually turn out for: 'I'm English, a West London boy through and through' he replied when questioned on the matter.

He perhaps inherited his speed from his mother, a former sprinter, but his game involved more than just pace: 'dynamism, speed, raw power and guts' is how Dick Best described him at an early age.

He made his try-scoring debut against Holland in 1998 before helping England to a home victory against world champions South Africa. The following year he helped England to the quarter-finals of the 1999 Rugby World Cup.

Luger returned to the side in the autumn of 2000 and scored possibly the most important try of his career in the final minute of a nail-biting encounter with world champions Australia. Trailing 15-19 in the eighth minute of injury time, Luger broke through to touch down a match-winning try that handed England their first win against the Wallabies in six attempts, giving Clive Woodward's side the belief that they might go on and conquer the world.

This they did in 2003 when Luger added tries to a Grand Slam winning 6 Nations campaign and helped his side lift the 2003 Rugby World Cup.

In all he earned thirty-eight caps and scored twenty-four tries.

BEN CHRISTOPHER COHEN (2000-2006)
Birthplace: Northampton
Position: Wing
Total Caps: 57
Calcutta Cups: 4
Triple Crowns: 2
Outright Championship Victories: 3
Grand Slams: 1
World Cup: 1

Ben Cohen came into the England side at a time when new tackle laws placed an emphasis on physicality. Cohen's size and strength, allied to solid hands and powerful running, allowed him to break tackles, get over the gain line and score tries.

He benefited from the wisdom of two former professional footballers in his immediate family. His uncle George was a member of England's 1966 World Cup-winning football team and taught him how to handle the pressure and remain patient and composed during big games.

His England debut was spectacular with two tries helping England to a 50-18 win over Ireland. He scored another against Wales and two more against Italy as England claimed the inaugural 6 Nations Championship. In 2001 Cohen helped England to a second consecutive outright championship before landing a Triple Crown in 2002.

In the Autumn of 2002 his sixteenth try in eighteen games gave England victory over the All-Blacks. Two more against Australia the following week and another against the Springboks a week later gave Cohen and England a unique treble.

In 2003 Cohen helped England to a Grand Slam, and victories in New Zealand and Australia, before starting in every game bar one of England's triumphant 2003 World Cup campaign.

Cohen continued to represent England until 2006 when he earned the last of his fifty-seven caps. His thirty-one tries place him equal second on the list of England's all-time record try-scorers.

Cohen has always suffered from tinnitus and his hearing deteriorated significantly during his career. Since retirement he has campaigned against homophobia and bullying via the Stand Up Foundation, which champions rugby as a vehicle of inclusivity, change and respect.

12

Inside Centre

FREDERICK HODGSON RUDD ALDERSON
(1891-1893)
Birthplace: Hartford
Position: Centre
Total Caps: 6
Calcutta Cups: 1
Triple Crowns: 1
Outright Championship Victories: 1
Grand Slams: n/a
World Cups: n/a

Fred Alderson brought pace, swerve and an accomplished kicking game when selected as a centre for his country in 1891. But it wasn't these skills that set him apart from his contemporaries. A strategist and natural leader, Alderson would regularly adapt his tactics on the field as games progressed and necessity dictated.

It was this latter quality that earned Alderson the rare distinction of being made captain on his debut, against Wales in 1891. He repaid the faith of the selectors by converting two tries and assisting his side to a 7-3 victory. He added another against Ireland and earned his fourth cap as captain at the start of the 1892 season.

He opened that campaign with a try and conversion that earned England a crushing 17-0 victory against Wales. His side went on to complete a clean sweep and Triple Crown for the first time since 1884.

Alderson's legendary 1892 side is the only side in 4/5/6 Nations history to have completed a full season without having conceded a single point.

Away from the field Alderson was a Headmaster. He earned the last of his six caps in 1893.

ANDREW 'DREWY' ERNEST STODDART (1885-1893)
Birthplace: Westoe
Position: Three-quarter
Total Caps: 10
Calcutta Cups: 1 retained
Triple Crowns: 0
Outright Championship Victories: 0
Grand Slams: n/a
World Cups: n/a

The man dubbed 'the most famous sportsman in Queen Victoria's empire' was born in County Durham in 1860. His sporting proficiency was quickly recognised and he became only the second man in history to captain England at both cricket and rugby.

Brilliant as a wing but equally adept among the centres, Stoddart was described as a 'dashing individualist' who, once in his stride, was practically unstoppable. A fierce competitor, he won many matches with the accuracy of his drop-kicking and is known to have regularly hurdled opponents in search of the try-line.

He was first selected for England in 1885. Between 1885 and 1889 he played in six tests without defeat. He then captained his side four times over the following four seasons.

Away from the national side he became the first captain of the Barbarians invitation side and also captained the side that would become the British and Irish Lions during their first tour in 1888. He is also on record as being the first player to have scored an underwater try for Harlequins on a waterlogged Chislehurst Common.

He reportedly played his last games for England with elastic knee caps on both knees, anklets on both ankles and a rubber bandage on his elbow.

The following is an extract from a poem printed in *Punch* magazine after Stoddart had captained the English cricket team to their ashes victory in 1894/5:

Then wrote the Queen of England,
Whose hand is blessed by God,
I must do something handsome,
For my dear victorious Stod'

EDWARD MYERS (1920-1925)
Birthplace: New York
Position: Centre
Total Caps: 18
Calcutta Cups: 4
Triple Crowns: 3
Outright Championship Victories: 3
Grand Slams: 3
World Cups: n/a

Eddie Myers was a Yorkshireman of few words who did most of his talking on the pitch. He first trialled for England in 1913 but would not make his debut until 1920. In between he was wounded three times during the First World War and received a Military Cross.

On his first start for England he set-up one try and scored another. His straight-line running from inside centre quickly became one of England's most effective weapons and helped deliver Grand Slams in 1921 and 1923.

His biggest challenge came the following season when he was asked to step into his former captain Dave Davies' shoes at fly-half. His subsequent performances were described as 'superb' by legendary former fly-half and captain Adrian Stoop. England won every game to secure a second consecutive Grand Slam and Myers rounded off the championship by landing a dropped goal and a try in the final fifteen minutes of the game against Scotland, which England went on to win 19-0.

In all he made eighteen appearances for his country of which fifteen were victories, retiring with an 86 per cent win rate.

LEONARD JAMES CORBETT (1921-1927)
Birthplace: Bristol
Position: Centre
Total Caps: 16
Calcutta Cups: 1
Triple Crowns: 3
Outright Championship Victories: 3
Grand Slams: 3
World Cups: n/a

Len Corbett was arguably the first English centre to adequately fill the shoes of the great Ronnie Poulton. Quick thinking, fast and skilful, he loved selling opponents the dummy and was credited with having the quickest hands in what was a truly outstanding England side.

He was selected just in time to play a part in the 1921 Grand Slam-winning team and was reselected at the start of the 1923 season. That year he scored a try and made two others in a comprehensive defeat of Ireland at Welford Road on the way to a second Grand Slam. He was ever present the following year, acting as try-scorer and provider in the opening match against Wales in Swansea, and Ireland in Belfast, as England completed their third Grand Slam in four seasons. In his final season, 1927, Corbett was given the England captaincy and led England to home victories against Wales and Ireland.

He retired with sixteen caps, having contributed to three Grand Slams. In later years he was the general manager of a chocolate factory and a sports correspondent for *The Sunday Times* newspaper.

CARL DOUGLAS AARVOLD (1928-1933)
Birthplace: Hartlepool
Position: Centre
Total Caps: 16
Calcutta Cups: 2
Triple Crowns: 1
Outright Championship Victories: 1
Grand Slams: 1
World Cups: n/a

Carl Aarvold was a back-row specialist whose lightning-quick acceleration was put to use on both wings and at inside and outside centre during his sixteen international caps.

He made his debut in 1928, helping England to a win over New South Wales. Later that year he played in every round of a season that would deliver England a fourth Grand Slam of the 1920s, under the leadership of Ronald Cove-Smith.

Over subsequent seasons Aarvold continued to make a nuisance of himself and was given the captaincy in 1932. His side managed to secure a share of the Championship that year with Aarvold himself scoring two tries in the decisive Calcutta Cup tie at Twickenham.

Aarvold had been called to the bar by the time he hung up his boots. He was made a judge in 1954 and in 1965 presided over the trial of the Ronnie and Reggie Kray.

JEFFREY BUTTERFIELD (1953-1959)
Birthplace: Heckmondwike
Position: Centre
Total Caps: 28
Calcutta Cups: 5 (+2 retained)
Triple Crowns: 2
Outright Championship Victories: 3
Grand Slams: 1
World Cups: n/a

Every now and then a back comes along whose ability to score and create spreads confidence through a side and fear through opponents. Jeff Butterfield had grown up watching Rugby League but as a Union player he had everything. An elusive powerful runner, with the ability to wrong foot an opponent before reaching them, he was praised by his teammates for his crash tackle, rhythmic pass, anticipation and split-second 'thrustfulness'.

He scored one try and set-up another on his England debut in 1953, before embarking on an unbroken run of twenty-eight consecutive caps, by the end of which he was England's most capped back. In his second match he scored again helping England to a convincing win against Scotland that saw England finish the season unbeaten and claim that year's championship.

The following season, a try against Ireland helped England on their way to the Triple Crown and in 1955 Butterfield made a try-scoring debut for the British and Irish Lions. He went on to score tries in three out of four Test matches against South Africa, sharing the series in the process.

An improving England hit on a winning formula in 1957. Low-scoring wins were secured against Wales, Ireland and France to set up a title decider against Scotland. Once again it was Butterfield who unlocked the opposition defence, sending his teammate over for a first-half try that set England on their way to a first Grand Slam in almost thirty years.

The following season England came within a whisker of repeating the trick but could only salvage a draw in their final game. Nevertheless they were outright champions for a second year running in a season in which they had also defeated visiting Australia.

1959 would be Butterfield's final season and he assumed the captaincy. Away from rugby he was a schoolteacher.

SIR CLIVE RONALD WOODWARD
(1980-1984)
Birthplace: Ely
Position: Centre
Total Caps: 21
Calcutta Cups: 2 (+1 retained)
Triple Crowns: 1
Outright Championship Victories: 1
Grand Slams: 1
World Cups: n/a

Clive Woodward was first selected for England in 1980. He came into the side at a time when centres generally relied upon their power to smash their way past opponents, but Woodward was different. Smaller than most in his position, he favoured enterprising, attacking runs, evading the tackle and drawing opponents away from his teammates. These skills were put to dramatic good use when he set up tries for Mike Slemen and John Carleton in the 1980 Calcutta Cup match, helping secure England's first Grand Slam in twenty-three years.

The 1980 side was characterised by dominant forward-play and had successfully ground out results against France, Ireland and Wales, but it was Woodward's attacking guile that made him the man of the match in a 30-18 victory against Scotland.

Woodward earned twenty-one caps in all and was later knighted after coaching England to victory in the 2003 Rugby World Cup.

WILLIAM DAVID CHARLES CARLING (1988-1997)
Birthplace: Bradford-Upon Avon
Position: Inside Centre
Total Caps: 72
Calcutta Cups: 8 (+1 retained)
Triple Crowns: 5
Outright Championship Victories: 4
Grand Slams: 3
World Cup: Finalist

Will Carling made his international debut at the age of twenty-two and, despite his tender years, stood out immediately both on and off the pitch. His presence convinced Geoff Cooke to make Carling England's youngest ever captain. Cooke was vindicated as Carling led his side to victory against a star-studded Australian side in the following match. Soon after Carling would become one of the most recognisable faces in world rugby.

Carling the player was a powerful running inside centre with the strength to break a line and the athleticism to evade a challenge. He formed an imposing international partnership with Jeremy Guscott that, allied to a quite formidable pack, brought England their first period of sustained success for many years.

In 1990 England came within a whisker of a Grand Slam but Carling galvanised his men and the following year they came back stronger. He 1991 and 1992 he became the first and, so far, only man to have captained England to back-to-back Grand Slams.

In between, his side recovered from early setbacks to reach a home World Cup Final in 1991 but, this time, could not overcome the Wallabies.

Triple Crowns followed in 1993 and 1994 before a third Grand Slam was added in 1995. An outright championship victory and Triple Crown followed in 1996 and a further Triple Crown was added in 1997 before Carling retired, so ending one of the most decorated careers in the history of English rugby.

Carling earned seventy-two caps in total and scored twelve tries. He remains the only Englishman to have captained his side to three Grand Slams.

PHILIP RANULPH DE GLANVILLE (1992-1999)
Birthplace: Loughborough
Position: Centre
Total Caps: 38
Calcutta Cups: 3
Triple Crowns: 3
Outright Championship Victories: 1
Grand Slams: 0
World Cups: Semi-Finalist

Inside centre Phil de Glanville had all the skills to make his breakthrough onto the international stage but found one of English rugby's finest ever centre-partnerships in Will Carling and Jeremy Guscott standing in his way.

But de Glanville had the determination and character to bide his time, his strength in the tackle and defensive work offering qualities that the other two lacked. He made his debut as a substitute winger in 1992 and two of his first three caps were victories over New Zealand and South Africa.

In 1995 he helped England reach the semi-final of the Rugby World Cup and made substitute appearances in England's outright championship win in 1996. He began the 1997 season as captain and led his side to a Triple Crown, scoring tries against Scotland and Wales along the way.

He contributed to another Triple Crown in 1998 before earning the last of his thirty-eight caps against South Africa in the quarter-final of the 1999 Rugby World Cup.

MICHAEL JOHN CATT (1994-2007)
Birthplace: Port Elizabeth
Position: Centre
Total Caps: 75
Calcutta Cups: 4
Triple Crowns: 5
Outright Championship Victories: 2
Grand Slams: 1
World Cups: 1

Mike Catt can lay claim to being the most versatile three-quarter in the history of English rugby. He considered himself a fly-half but played most of his rugby for England at either full-back, inside centre or on the wing. In every case he excelled.

Despite the different attributes required for each position he brought an aggressive South-African approach to them all. Like his name implies, he was agile, but also an incisive runner, hard tackler and reliable under the high ball.

He was born in Port Elizabeth to an English mother and earned his first England cap in 1994. He made his first start in 1995 and helped England achieve a Grand Slam and reach a World Cup semi-final.

The following year he helped England retain the Championship as well as winning Triple Crowns in 1996, 1997 and 1998. He reached a World Cup Quarter-final in 1999 and helped England claim the Championship again in 2000 and 2001.

In 2003 he contributed to the most successful season in the history of English rugby, starting in the semi-final and making a substitute's appearance in the final of England's 2003 Rugby World Cup campaign.

He remained an active member of the squad when England reached a second consecutive World Cup Final in 2007.

In all Catt made seventy-five appearances for his country.

The 1990-1995 Team

Will Carling is the only Englishman to have captained his side to three Grand Slams. His tenure stretched from 1988 to 1996, a period of sustained excellence during which England were able to draw upon the likes of Brian Moore, Wade Dooley, Jason Leonard, Rory Underwood, Rob Andrew, Dean Richards and Jeremy Guscott, outstanding individual performers who formed the collective nucleus of one of England's greatest sides.

England v Ireland match programme, 1988.

The Will Carling era, as it has come to be known, perhaps began on the 19 March 1988. Carling himself had made his debut earlier that year and had made waves with his powerful running from inside his own half. Still the season had not been a success and very little was expected of an England side that faced Ireland in the final round of a disappointing 5 Nations campaign.

Matters were made worse during the first half when, trailing 0-3, captain Nigel Melville suffered a broken leg that would mean the end of his international career. Sensing the concern of his teammates the skilful scrum-half waved them away and is reported to have issued one simple command: 'say it with tries'.

The words proved inspirational and England reacted by touching down six times without response. Two came from the irrepressible Rory Underwood and three came from Chris Oti, playing at Twickenham for the first time. The fans responded and began singing 'Swing Low Sweet Chariot', a song that had previously been mostly confined to the locker room. It has been England's unofficial rugby anthem ever since.

Later that year, England team manager Geoff Cooke made Carling his captain and England stunned the world by recording a 28-19 victory over Australia. A much improved 5 Nations season followed. Dewi Morris partnered Andrew in midfield while further back Carling had found the rapier to his axe in the shape of Jeremy Guscott, whose quick feet and agile stride would deliver ten tries in his first nine starts.

While this was taking place among the backs, England's pack was rapidly becoming one of the world's best with a spine that included Brian Moore,

England team, 1991.

Wade Dooley, Paul Ackford and Peter Winterbottom. The signs were there to suggest that England would soon be serious championship contenders.

So it proved, and free-scoring England began the following season with crushing victories against Ireland, France and Wales, scoring no fewer than eleven tries in the process. It seemed a Grand Slam was there for the taking and only Scotland remained in their way. However with the newspapers rightly hailing England's new-found attacking prowess, scant attention was paid to an improving Scotland side that had also won all of its games.

Amid a swirling cauldron of passion, noise and intensity Scotland never allowed England a grip on the game. The Grand Slam was lost and English pride was punctured. But contained within that small group of men who had it in their power to make amends, there was a burning resolve that it should not happen again. Murrayfield was to be the catalyst for sustained success.

For all the verve and endeavour among the backs, Team Manager Geoff Cooke had observed that his pack had made further improvement. A young Jason Leonard stood alongside Moore while Mike Teague and Dean Richards stood alongside Winterbottom in the back row. This gave England game-plan options.

The following season England opted to turn the screw. Gone was the flamboyant attacking play and cricket-scores of the previous year. In its place controlled possession-rugby and wins, against Wales, Scotland and Ireland. Cooke had learned that unlike some of his opponents England would never win easily. Defeating England meant too much to the opposition and so the only way to guarantee wins was to dominate the field. A second consecutive Grand Slam decider followed, this time against France at Twickenham.

England v France match programme, 1991.

Bill McLaren's commentary notes for the meeting between England and Scotland in 1991.

With the prize so near, England once more wobbled, Serge Blanco initiating a move from behind his own try-line that gave France impetus and an early lead. But this time England stuck to their guns and, with the wounds of Murrayfield perhaps still raw, got over the line with the help of a try from Rory Underwood and points from Andrew and Simon Hodgkinson.

As Grand Slam holders, Carling's England went into a home Rugby World Cup with realistic hopes of winning rugby's ultimate prize, but defeat to New Zealand in the pool stage blunted that ambition. Wins against Italy and USA followed and England were into the quarter-finals where they would face France.

Three successive wins against the French gave England a psychological advantage but the French were at home. A bruising affair followed typified by the forthright resistance of the English pack to wave after wave of attacking French scrums and no-holds-barred tackling from the likes of Micky Skinner. In the end a Will Carling try made the game safe for England and paved the way to the semi-finals.

Rob Andrew's nerve settled a closely matched encounter with Scotland and England were set to contest their first Rugby World Cup final. In the lead up outspoken Australian wing David Campese expressed his side's apprehension about facing Brian Moore's well-oiled forward machine by almost daring his opponents to adopt a more attacking approach for the final. England perhaps rose to the bait despite Australia's proven ability in converting possession into points.

England came off second best in the first half before mounting a spirited second-half comeback that brought them within touching distance of the Wallabies. It was not to be but reaching a World Cup final was a high watermark of sorts for Carling's side.

On the back of their disappointment England were drawn at Murrayfield for the opening encounter of the 1992 Championship. They were champions but faced a strong Scotland side who had proven to be England's closest 5 Nations rivals. The home side also had the extra motivation of seeking to exact revenge for their Semi-final defeat the previous autumn.

After the defeat against Australia, England might have been forgiven a degree of lethargy coming into the game. As it transpired self-pity did not feature in the psychological make-up of the side and neither did mercy. Dean Richards had not initially been selected for the match but ended up its standout performer in a 25-7 victory.

This inbuilt resilience would carry England throughout the competition. In their next match they outclassed Ireland with six tries from Underwood, Guscott, Morris and Jonathan Webb. Webb would finish the season with a record sixty-seven points as England recorded their first back-to-back Grand Slam since William Wavell Wakefield's side in 1924, and most dominant season since Norman Wodehouse captained the side to its first Slam way back in 1913.

Only a magnificent try from Ireland's Simon Geoghegan prevented a third in four seasons in 1994 by which time new faces such as Neil Back, Kyran Bracken and Martin Johnson had been added to the side.

In 1995 the third Slam was secured and although the green shoots of the next great England side were already in evidence it was Carling, Andrew, Guscott, Moore, Leonard and the Underwood brothers who steered the ship home once more.

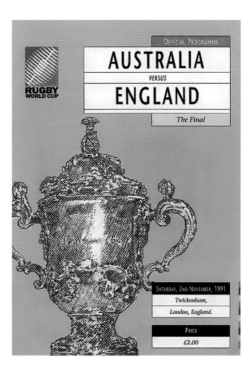

Right: England v Australia match programme, 1991.

Below: England dressing room, 1995.

13

Outside Centre

RICHARD EVISON LOCKWOOD DICKY
Birthplace: Crigglestone
Position: Three-quarter
Total Caps: 14
Calcutta Cups: 1 (+1 retained)
Triple Crowns: 1
Outright Championship Victories: 1
Grand Slams: n/a
World Cups: n/a

Dicky Lockwood spearheaded an influx of working-class rugby players who began to impact on the national side as the game grew rapidly in popularity among industrial towns and cities of the north in the late 1880s.

At only 5 feet 4 ½ inches it would have been easy to overlook Lockwood but such was his attacking potency and unpredictable cat-like runs from deep in his own half that quickly caught the eye of all who saw him.

He made his debut for Dewsbury at the age of sixteen before being called up for Yorkshire, the North and then England at just nineteen. Far from being overawed by his new surroundings, Lockwood is credited with having introduced the four three-quarter system, first to Yorkshire, then to England.

In 1892 he helped England to the Triple Crown and in 1894 was given the England captaincy. A master-showman and born entertainer, in his pomp he was described as 'Little Dick, the World's Wonder'. He earned fourteen caps in total.

JOHN GUY GILBERNE BIRKETT (1906-1912)
Birthplace: Richmond
Position: Centre
Total Caps: 21
Calcutta Cups: 3
Triple Crowns: 0
Outright Championship Victories: 1
Grand Slams: 0
World Cups: n/a

John Birkett's father had become the first international try-scorer in the history of rugby, against Scotland in 1871. In 1909 John went close to emulating his father's feat by becoming the first try-scorer at Twickenham Stadium.

Birkett was the axe in a classic 'axe and rapier' centre combination with clubmate Ronnie Poulton. His powerful running was frequently described as 'bullocking' and he was the bane of opposition defences. In all he scored ten tries in twenty-one international appearances

He was first selected for England in 1906 and captained the side five times including in the final game of the 1910 season when his determined running brought him two tries in a 14-5 victory. The result brought England a first Championship in eighteen years.

During the First World War, Birkett served in the Royal Field Artillery and his gallantry was mentioned in despatches eighteen times.

RONALD 'RONNIE' WILLIAM POULTON* (1909-1914)
Birthplace: Oxford
Position: Centre
Total Caps: 17
Calcutta Cups: 3
Triple Crowns: 2
Outright Championship Victories: 3
Grand Slams: 2
World Cups: n/a

Inset: Ronnie Poulton's England Rose.

Ronnie Poulton is often described as having had a swerving running style when, in his own words, he ran straight and trusted his swinging arms and hips to ensure that opponents would swerve out of his way. Either way his 'corkscrew running' style mesmerised opponents and earned him a reputation as one of the best players that England has ever produced.

He was first selected in 1909 and the following season played on the wing during Twickenham's first ever international, helping his side to a victory that would contribute to England's first Championship victory since 1892. The following season he was switched to his favourite position of outside centre and in 1913 played a starring role in a campaign that landed England's first Grand Slam.

In 1914 he was made captain – an act which seemed to spur Poulton to even greater heights. A quite brilliant campaign followed, by the end of which English rugby fans were convinced that Poulton was without question the finest rugby player in the world.

As captain Poulton's trickery and invention saw him put in man of the match performances in each of England's first three games to land his side the Triple Crown. In the final game, against France, a second consecutive Grand Slam was secured with a crushing 39-13 victory. England scored nine tries with Poulton, who had simply outclassed his opponents, personally scoring four.

Later that year Poulton enlisted with the Royal Berkshire Regiment. The following year he was shot and killed by sniper fire in a trench south of Ypres at the age of twenty-five. Contemporaries claim that Poulton had no enemies and many of his company were reported to have wept at the dawn stand-to the morning after his death.

A beautiful player, a character of the highest integrity, one of the loveliest and the best…he might have stood as a symbol of the heart of England…of the golden young men who died faithfully and fearlessly in a war where much that was of value beyond price in an imperfect world perished, too.

A. A. Thomson

* Poulton changed his name to Palmer in 1914 and is now often referred to as Poulton-Palmer.

HAROLD MEADOWS LOCKE (1923-1927)
Birthplace: Birkenhead
Position: Centre
Total Caps: 12
Calcutta Cups: 2
Triple Crowns: 2
Outright Championship Victories: 2
Grand Slams: 2
World Cups: n/a

Harold Locke had been a fly-half as a schoolboy but later converted to centre. Fast and with quick hands he specialised in getting the ball out wide as fast as possible. A selfless distributor, but also a thinker who worked hard on his technique away from the field, Locke saw it as his role to lay on tries for his wing-three-quarter.

He was first selected for England in 1923 and helped his side to a Grand Slam the same year. The following year he struck up a partnership with Len Corbett that resulted in a try for Locke against Wales and two more for Jake Jacobs against France. A win against Scotland meant that Locke had helped England to back-to-back Grand Slams in his first two seasons.

Locke would earn a further seven caps, retiring in 1927 with twelve in total.

PETER CRANMER (1934-1938)
Birthplace: Birmingham
Position: Centre
Total Caps: 16
Calcutta Cups: 3
Triple Crowns: 2
Outright Championship Victories: 2
Grand Slams: n/a
World Cups: n/a

Peter Cranmer was a first class cricketer and rugby player and his period as an England international coincided with the side's most successful spell of the 1930s.

While sometimes described as an orthodox running centre, Cranmer had a lot more to his game than straight lines. His ability to crash through opponents and quick hands helped set up one of English rugby's most celebrated victories, against New Zealand in 1936. He was also a stout tackler and magnificent in defence when called upon.

He was introduced to the side at the age of twenty-one, in 1934, and immediately helped his side to an unbeaten season in which they claimed the Triple Crown and outright championship having conceded only six points.

He landed a dropped goal against Scotland in 1935. In 1936 he landed another dropped goal and laid on tries for both Hal Sever and Alexander Obolensky to secure England's first victory against New Zealand, in what was perhaps Cranmer's most accomplished performance.

In 1937 Cranmer and his team secured the Triple Crown again with another clean sweep. Grand Slams were not on the table in the 1930s due to France's expulsion from the tournament, but three narrow victories were secured with Cranmer England's chief attacking outlet.

In 1938 Cranmer assumed the role of captain and signed off with a crushing 36-14 victory away to Ireland. He earned sixteen caps in all.

During the Second World War he served in Egypt and Burma before becoming a journalist and BBC broadcaster.

MICHAEL PHILIP WESTON (1960-1968)
Birthplace: Durham
Position: Centre
Total Caps: 29
Calcutta Cups: 4
Triple Crowns: 1
Outright Championship Victories: 1
Grand Slams: 0
World Cups: n/a

Mike Weston started out as a fly-half but converted to centre where his quick hands regularly facilitated the forward runs of his teammates. Quietly effective rather than bombastic, he was a useful foil for both England and the touring British and Irish Lions of 1962 and 1966. He was particularly strong in defence and his calmness under pressure assisted in his nerveless place kicking.

He made his debut in an England jersey in 1960, helping England defeat a strong Welsh side in the process. His try against France meant that his side remained unbeaten and earned a share of that year's 5 Nations Championship. He remained in the side until 1963 when England won the Championship outright.

Later that year he replaced Richard Sharp as captain and led his side on a tour of New Zealand and Australia. He was in and out of the side over the following four seasons but returned as captain in his original position of fly-half in 1968, claiming the Calcutta Cup in Edinburgh in his final game.

In all, Weston earned twenty-nine caps before a foot injury ended his career.

PAUL WILLIAM DODGE (1978-1985)
Birthplace: Leicester
Position: Centre
Total Caps: 32
Calcutta Cups: 4 (+2 retained)
Triple Crowns: 1
Outright Championship Victories: 1
Grand Slams: 1
World Cups: n/a

Paul Dodge believed in quick hands above all else. He thrived on the quick ball and specialised in releasing wingers. He also brought a power game to the midfield which was hard but fair.

He was called up for England in 1978 and scored his first international try against Scotland the same year. In 1980 his successful Leicester Tigers midfield partnership with Clive Woodward was transferred onto the international stage with instant results as England claimed their first Grand Slam since 1957.

In 1983 he helped his side defeat the All-Blacks at Twickenham. He rounded off his international career by captaining the side throughout the 1985 season. In total Dodge won thirty-two caps including seven as captain.

JEREMY CLAYTON GUSCOTT (1989-1999)
Birthplace: Bath
Position: Centre
Total Caps: 65
Calcutta Cups: 7
Triple Crowns: 6
Outright Championship Victories: 4
Grand Slams: 3
World Cups: Finalist

Jeremy Guscott worked as a bricklayer, bus driver and representative of British Gas, before joining the first wave of professional rugby players in 1995. By then he had long since established himself as one of English rugby's finest proponents of running rugby.

Guscott specialised in running inventive lines from all angles, igniting attacks and cutting ribbons out of his opponents' defensive line. His club-side Bath enjoyed a prolonged period of domestic dominance with him in the side. His debut for the national side in 1989 brought him a hat-trick of tries, setting him off on an international career that would last for over a decade.

He landed ten tries in his first nine matches and helped England to Grand Slams in 1991 and 1992. In the quarter-final of the 1991 Rugby World Cup it was Guscott's explosive running and intelligent movement that lead to Underwood's try, which paved England's route to the final.

Guscott remained a potent force as well as a match-winner late into his career, adding another Grand Slam in 1995, an outright championship in 1996, and Triple Crowns in 1997 and 1998. In 1997 he landed the dropped goal that secured a series victory against South Africa for the British and Irish Lions.

He played in the 1995 and 1999 Rugby World Cups before retiring with sixty-five caps. *The Sunday Times* veteran rugby correspondent Stephen Jones described Guscott as the greatest all-round centre he had seen.

WILLIAM JOHN HEATON GREENWOOD (199 7-2004)
Birthplace: Blackburn
Position: Centre
Total Caps: 55
Calcutta Cups: 5
Triple Crowns: 5
Outright Championship Victories: 2
Grand Slams: 1
World Cups: 1

Although predominantly an inside centre, superstition dictated that Will Greenwood only ever wore the number 13 jersey for England.

As the son of former England flanker Dick Greenwood, Will might have been expected to excel as a schoolboy. Instead he couldn't get into his school team. Never deterred, Greenwood kept plugging away until eventually he added a degree of bulk to his slender frame and began to express himself.

A willing runner with the creative spark to unlock a defence Greenwood was also extremely effective in breaching the gain line, setting-up points and scoring tries. So competent did Greenwood become in the latter department that at the end of his career his thirty-one tries for England saw him second on the all-time leader board.

Those tries came across fifty-five caps, the first of which was acquired in a home draw with Australia in 1997. At a time when England had an abundance of exceptional centres, Greenwood formed effective partnerships with Mike Catt and Mike Tindall, among others. As a player who relished the big occasions, his fortunes prospered in tandem with the national side.

In 2001 he scored a hat-trick of tries against Wales in the Millenium Stadium, helping his side to that year's championship in the process. He played in every game of England's 2003 Grand Slam success, scoring tries against Wales and Ireland.

It was Greenwood's vital try against Wales that allowed England to progress to the semi-finals of the 2003 Rugby World Cup. An incessant communicator whose instruction informed Jonny Wilkinson throughout the tournament, it was he who was first to embrace the fly-half after he had landed the points that would deliver England the tournament for the first time.

He finished the tournament as England's joint top try-scorer, despite returning home during the group stage to be present for the birth of his second son.

The last of his fifty-five caps came against Australia in 2004. In his career Greenwood didn't lose a single Test-match against Scotland or Wales.

MICHAEL JAMES TINDALL (2000-2011)
Birthplace: Wakefield
Position: Centre
Total Caps: 75
Calcutta Cups: 5
Triple Crowns: 2
Outright Championship Victories: 4
Grand Slams: 1
World Cups: 1

Clive Woodward described Mike Tindall as 'the rock' upon whom his 2003 all-conquering side were built. A tremendously powerful line breaker, he supplied the muscle to a midfield trio that included Jonny Wilkinson and Will Greenwood.

He was called into the 1999 World Cup squad as a replacement for the injured Jeremy Guscott, but would have to wait until 2000 for his first cap. He marked it with a try against Ireland in a campaign that brought England the inaugural 6 Nations title.

The following year he played a bit-part in a successful defence of the title before becoming a regular in a side that, in 2002, captured a Triple Crown before recording consecutive victories against New Zealand, Australia and South Africa.

By now Tindall commanded the respect of the dressing room and his two tries helped England to a Grand Slam in 2003. Later that year he would play in every round of the 2003 Rugby World Cup including the final against Australia which he helped England to win.

He featured in each of the following three seasons but missed the 2007 Rugby World Cup through injury.

As the breakdown became a more crucial feature of the game Tindall added ground skills to his game and, in 2010, turned over Australian ball on his own line to set in motion a move that supplied Chris Ashton with an 80-yard touchdown.

In 2011 he played seven times as captain, lifting the Calcutta Cup and helping England to a first outright championship since 2003. Later that year he captained England during the 2011 World Cup campaign, which ended at the quarter-final stage. He earned seventy-five caps in all.

14

Right-wing

FREDERICK ERNEST CHAPMAN (1910-1914)
Birthplace: South Shields
Position: Wing
Total Caps: 7
Calcutta Cups: 2
Triple Crowns: 1
Outright Championship Victories: 2
Grand Slams: 1
World Cups: n/a

Fred Chapman first came to the attention of selectors when he put two tries past an England-elect side in the final trial match before Twickenham's first international fixture in 1910. The selectors promptly made a quick U-turn and promoted Chapman to the full side. It was the correct decision.

Thin but wiry Chapman was a strong runner, difficult to stop when allowed to get up to speed. He was also one of the earliest proponents of the side-step and foxed many an opponent in this way.

Chapman is in the records books for having scored the first international try at Twickenham Stadium and did so within thirty seconds of the kick-off. His score set England on their way claiming their first Championship victory since 1892.

He returned to the side in 1914 to play a part in securing a Grand Slam in the final season before the First World War.

Although he only played seven times for England he won on 6 of those occasions, retiring with a 93 per cent win rate.

CYRIL 'KID' NELSON LOWE (1913-1923)
Birthplace: Holbeach
Position: Winger
Total Caps: 25
Calcutta Cups: 6
Triple Crowns: 4
Outright Championship Victories: 4
Grand Slams: 4
World Cups: n/a

Cyril Lowe was 5 feet 6 inches and weighed 8.5 stone but that didn't prevent him from becoming arguably England's most decorated wing of all time.

Lightning quick, with a predator's eye for the try-line and the footwork to exploit gaps that weren't even there, a teammate once described Lowe 'slither(ing) past two or three defenders like a ghost'. Fiercely determined Lowe contributed almost as much in defence as attack, locking onto opponents and bringing them to earth when danger arose.

He made the first of an unbroken twenty-five caps as part of the 1913 side which secured England's first Grand Slam. The following season England made it back-to-back Grand Slams with Lowe contributing eight tries, a record that has never been surpassed by any player in 4/5/6 Nations history.

During the First World War Lowe is credited with having shot down thirty German aircraft for which he received the Military Cross and Distinguished Flying Cross. His exploits in the cockpit are believed to have been the inspiration for W. E. Johns character 'Biggles'.

He returned to the national side when international rugby reconvened in 1920 and was instrumental in securing two further Grand Slams in 1921 and 1923. The eighteen tries that he scored for his country remained an English record when he passed away at the age of ninety-one in 1983.

HOWARD CARSTON CATCHESIDE (1924-1927)
Birthplace: Sunderland
Position: Winger
Total Caps: 8
Calcutta Cups: 1
Triple Crowns: 1
Outright Championship Victories: 1
Grand Slams: 1
World Cups: n/a

Percy Park's Carston Catcheside became only the second player in twelve years to play on the English right-wing when he was selected to replace legendary Kid Lowe in 1924. His selection had become mandatory after he scored tries in each of that season's three trial matches. The same year he became the first English player to score in every round of the championship, scoring six tries in all and helping England to one of the most dominant Grand Slams in 5 Nations history.

He was left out of the 1925 side before being selected as a full-back in 1926 and twice more in his favoured right-wing position in 1927.

In 1936 Catcheside was appointed to the England selectors committee where he was eventually made chairman, a position he held until 1962. He served in both world wars, eventually attaining the rank of colonel.

In 1924 William Wavell Wakefield claimed that Catcheside had to be hauled aboard their steamer as it left Dublin harbour, having arrived late!

PRINCE ALEXANDER 'OBO' SERGEEVICH OBOLENSKY (1936)
Birthplace: St Petersburg
Position: Wing
Total Caps: 4
Calcutta Cups: 1
Triple Crowns: 0
Outright Championship Victories: 0
Grand Slams: n/a
World Cups: n/a

For a player to have made it on to these lists with only four caps he would have to have done something pretty special. Prince Alexander Obolensky did exactly that on the 4 January 1936. It was his debut and it was England's first ever victory over New Zealand.

Obolensky was born into Russian nobility in 1916. The following year the Bolshevik Revolution would drive his family out of their native land, the young Prince arriving in England as a baby in 1917.

The Flying Prince first came to the attention of the England selectors while a student at Oxford University where his try-scoring exploits earned him a call-up. There was a snag however: Obolensky was a Russian. British citizenship was arranged but the national debate over his legitimacy to wear the rose ensued. The Prince of Wales is purported to have asked Obolensky 'by what right do you presume to play for England?' as he lined up at Twickenham.

Obolensky silenced any critics by scoring two outstanding tries and handing New Zealand their first defeat at the hands of England. It was a scintillating cameo that had a positive impact on the English attitude to sporting inclusiveness and nationhood for many years to come.

But Obolensky's star was one that burned all too bright and all too fast. In 1938 he answered the call of his adopted homeland by joining the Royal Air Force Auxiliary and was tragically killed in a flight-training exercise in 1940.

PETER BARRIE JACKSON (1956-1963)
Birthplace: Birmingham
Position: Winger
Total Caps: 20
Calcutta Cups: 4
Triple Crowns: 1
Outright Championship Victories: 3
Grand Slams: 1
World Cups: n/a

Peter Jackson was a proponent of the art of elusive running. He was likened to a Russian ballet dancer in his ability to slip past opponents, and his most celebrated moment came when he did exactly that in the final minute of a bruising match against Australia in 1958. With the scores level at 6-6, England were effectively playing with thirteen men, having lost two key players to injury and concussion. With time running out a determined run from Jackson took him around three defenders and in at the corner flag to the delight of the home supporters.

He had made his test debut two years earlier as a member of Eric Evans' improving side. In 1957 he put in two try-scoring performances against Ireland and France to help his side to their first Grand Slam in almost thirty years. England defended their title the following season and Jackson was still making a nuisance of himself in 1963 when he played in every game of Richard Sharp's championship-winning season.

For England he scored six tries in twenty appearances. On the 1959 British and Irish Lions tour of New Zealand he managed nineteen in eighteen appearances. His Lions teammate Tony O'Reilly summed him up thus: 'The supreme example of the great joy of rugby, which is running with the ball.'

PETER JOHN SQUIRES (1973-1979)
Birthplace: Ripon
Position: Winger
Total Caps: 29
Calcutta Cups: 4 (+1 retained)
Triple Crowns: 0
Outright Championship Victories: 0
Grand Slams: 0
World Cups: n/a

England hadn't won a championship game in two seasons when Peter Squires received his international call-up. He put that right by beating France on his debut. Later the same year he would go over for a try in Auckland to set England on the way to a first away win over New Zealand. On their return home they defeated Australia at Twickenham.

By now the fleet-footed, skilful Yorkshireman had embarked on an almost unbroken run of appearances that would stretch throughout the 1970s. Although they were years of underachievement for England, Squires was a constant thorn in opposition sides, landing six tries in all.

By the time of his retirement in 1979 Squires had become England's most capped winger, with twenty-nine appearances in total.

JOHN CARLETON (1979-1984)
Birthplace: Orrell
Position: Winger
Total Caps: 26
Calcutta Cups: 2 (+1 retained)
Triple Crowns: 1
Outright Championship Victories: 1
Grand Slams: 1
World Cups: n/a

John Carleton made his international debut on his twenty-fourth birthday, against New Zealand at Twickenham in 1979. A right-wing specialist, he had come to the attention of the selectors by defeating the All-Blacks in sensational style with a representative side from the North of England.

With exceptional speed and the ability to finish off try scoring moves, Carleton was also defensively adept, operating as an auxiliary full-back as and when required.

In 1980 he landed a hat-trick of tries against Scotland in the decisive game of a season in which England claimed her first Grand Slam since 1957. He later played a part in home wins over Australia and New Zealand in 1982 and 1983. In all he scored seven tries in twenty-six appearances.

ANTHONY UNDERWOOD (1992-1998)
Birthplace: Ipoh
Position: Winger
Total Caps: 27
Calcutta Cups: 4
Triple Crowns: 2
Outright Championship Victories: 1
Grand Slams: 1
World Cups: Semi-Finalist

Tony Underwood's calmness and poise often allowed him to sneak, undetected, into dangerous areas of play from where his explosive speed was put to good use.

Off the field Underwood was equally serene, choosing not to drink and committing himself wholly to being the best rugby player that he could be.

He made his international debut in 1992 and scored on his Twickenham debut the same year, helping England to come from behind to defeat South Africa in the process.

His try against Ireland and two against France helped England achieve a Grand Slam in 1995, and he scored two more in helping his side to the semi-final of the 1995 Rugby World Cup.

He returned to the side in 1997 and added a further three tries, helping England to a Triple Crown along the way before earning his final cap in 1998.

In all, he scored thirteen tries in twenty-seven tests.

AUSTIN SEAN HEALEY (1997-2003)
Birthplace: Wallasey
Position: Winger
Total Caps: 51
Calcutta Cups: 3
Triple Crowns: 2
Outright Championship Victories: 2
Grand Slams: 0
World Cups: Quarter-finals

Austin Healey was a natural footballer who could make an impact anywhere among the backs. By trade he was undoubtedly a scrum-half but England's strength in depth in this position meant that Healey earned most of his England caps on the wing. This didn't bother Healey who when questioned on the matter replied 'I'll play anywhere'.

His free running and expressive rugby allied to his abundance of confidence caused regular problems for England's opponents during his six international seasons. His propensity to chat back to opponents had him branded the Leicester Lip.

He earned his first call-up in 1997 and contributed to back-to-back Triple Crowns in his first two seasons. In 1999 he made try scoring contributions to England's run to the quarter-finals of the 1999 Rugby World Cup. A further five tries helped England to the 2000 6 Nations Championship and three more helped Healey and England repeat the trick the following year.

In all Healey scored fifteen tries in fifty-one appearances for his country.

NAME: MARK JOHN CUETO (2004-2011)
Birthplace: Workington
Position: Wing
Total Caps: 55
Calcutta Cups: 3 (+1 retained)
Triple Crowns: 0
Outright Championship Victories: 1
Grand Slams: 0
World Cups: Finalist

Mark Cueto didn't really start playing rugby until he was seventeen, but from that point on his progression was rapid. A fast, confident wing, with a predator's eye for the try-line, he was first selected for England in 2004.

As world champions shorn of some of their most influential players England were in a period of sometimes painful adjustment. Cueto however bucked the trend by scoring eight tries in his first eight appearances.

In 2007 Cueto helped England into a second consecutive World Cup Final and went desperately close to scoring on the biggest stage of all. Debate still rages as to whether or not his foot was in touch. Cueto himself insists it was not.

He was absent from the team the following year but returned in 2009 with a try against Italy and another in a memorable win against France.

In 2011 Cueto would help England to a first outright championship since 2003. Later that year he scored a hat-trick of tries against Romania in the group stages of the 2011 World Cup and another in England's unsuccessful quarter-final against France.

The quarter-final was to be the last of his fifty-five caps in which he scored twenty tries.

In 2015 he retired from the game, having scored more tries in the English Premiership than any other player.

The 2000-2003 Team

When Clive Woodward became England team manager in 1997 he inherited a number of outstanding rugby players in the peak years of their careers. Jason Leonard, having transformed Will Carling's side, had already acquired enough accolades to be ranked alongside the all-time greats of English rugby. Martin Johnson wasn't too far behind and Kyran Bracken and Mike Catt also had achieved success with the national side. In addition, Lawrence Dallaglio, Neil Back and Matt Dawson had made useful starts to their international careers and were hungry for more.

England dressing room as during Clive Woodward's management.

Throughout the 1990s England had enjoyed a sustained upper hand over most of their European rivals but so far had always fallen short in achieving consistent success over the giants of the southern hemisphere. This was a pattern that Woodward was determined to change but defeat to the Springboks at the quarter-final stage of the 1999 Rugby World Cup made it clear that further weapons would be required to bolster his squad in order to do so.

Waiting on the bench was a young fly-half by the name of Jonny Wilkinson, who had made his international debut in 1998 at the age of nineteen. Wilkinson had already shown sufficient maturity on the field to hint at his promise, and a near faultless consistency with the boot was one weapon that Woodward was keen to utilise. He would be deployed behind a settled back row of Back, Dallaglio and Richard Hill, a unit whose mastery of the breakdown was always likely to produce kicking opportunities for the young fly-half.

Despite their defeat Woodward insisted that England were a better side than South Africa and they went some way towards proving so by defeating them the following year in Bloemfontein. Even so, isolated victories against southern-hemisphere sides were nothing new and England would need to beat them consistently to reach the heights that Woodward and his players aspired to.

In 2000, in the dying seconds of an autumn international against Australia Woodward's side did something so special that it suggested to all that, just maybe, the narrative had shifted. It had been a hard-fought game in which England had failed to convert possession into points. Australia were relaxed; England hadn't beaten them in five prior attempts, and expected to run the clock down while defending a seven point cushion. The cushion was reduced to four in the final seconds of normal time before a full eight minutes of relentless pressure from the home side.

With the crowd on their feet Dan Luger hunted down a hopeful chip from Iain Balshaw in the dying moments. Somehow he got between the Australian defence found the ball and touched down for a score that had the home support in raptures. Wilkinson converted and England had beaten the world champions.

A second consecutive 6 Nations title followed in 2001 before South Africa and Australia returned to Twickenham in the autumn. Meanwhile the developing side had been further bolstered by the try-scoring exploits of inside centre Will Greenwood and wing Ben Cohen in addition to the explosive genius of Rugby League convert Jason Robinson.

Robinson had played at the highest level as a Rugby League player, representing England in a World Cup Final in 1995. His seamless conversion to rugby union gifted England a player who could run from deep and whose elusive running supplied a platform for attack. In the end though, it was the English pack that set up two comfortable victories and by 2002 England had established themselves as a world-class outfit that need fear no one.

Challenges still remained however. Despite winning the 6 Nations championship two years running, single defeats meant that the Grand Slam eluded them. In 2002, defeat in Paris, handed the championship to France. England would need to find extra consistency to achieve their goals and there was also the simple matter of a certain team in black.

New Zealand came to Twickenham in the autumn to face a confident England side with an established game plan. An early try from Lewis Moody and a magnificent chip and chase solo try from Jonny Wilkinson saw England into a comfortable 31-17 lead. In the end it was a little closer; nonetheless England conquered the last of their foes and proved to themselves that they now had the required personnel to be considered the best in the world.

Clive Woodward however did not sit still, and recognising the importance of having a winning mentality he instigated a discipline known as 'Thinking Correctly Under Pressure' or T-CUP for short. These reserves were in evidence as England held off the All-Blacks' late fightback and would be called upon even more directly against Australia. Trailing by twelve points as the game approached its final quarter, England remained calm and focused, overhauling the Aussies with the help of a late Ben Cohen try to win 32-31. Having defeated Australia for a third successive time they then demolished the Springboks and went into 2003 as the world's number one team.

Many were now beginning to talk in terms of this being England's finest ever side, so Woodward turned his attention to the squad. Solid contributions and rejuvenated form from experienced players such as Paul Grayson, Graham Rowntree, Phil Vickery, Julian White and Danny Grewcock, allied to the emergence of new talent like Ben Kay, Lewis Moody, Steve Thompson, Mike Tindall, Josh Lewsey and Joe Worsley gave England strength in depth as well as competition for places. All would be necessary as England entered the all-important calendar year of 2003.

England v Italy match programme, 2003.

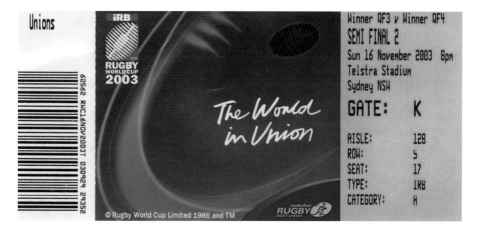

England v France match ticket, 2003.

Whereas before England had an upper hand over their 6 Nations rivals they now enjoyed an advantage approaching dominance. One by one their rivals were brushed aside to set up a Grand Slam decider with Ireland in Dublin. Martin Johnson's obstinate refusal to move in advance of the national anthems was indicative of his team's mindset. Contrary to earlier nearmisses, this time England were focused and determined. They ran out 42-6 winners. The Grand Slam was theirs.

Having beaten all of the southern hemisphere sides at home they now had to show that they could do so on the road. A bruising encounter with New Zealand in Wellington supplied the first opportunity and despite being reduced to thirteen men, with both Dallaglio and Back sent from the field, England held on to record a 15-13 victory. This first victory in New Zealand for thirty years meant that England would cross the Tasman Sea with confidence as they went in search of a first ever victory in Australia. It duly arrived. With Robinson in sparkling form the Wallabies proved no match for Woodward's side, who ran out 25-14 winners.

That England were now the number one side in the world was indisputable but the ultimate prize remained to be won. Woodward's task was to maintain the balance of the side and make the difficult decisions in advance of the tournament. To this end several players such as Austin Healy and Graham Rowntree, who had contributed directly to England's ascendency, were left behind. Those who remained knew that they must deliver.

England cruised through the group stage without serious challenge. Despite not playing their best rugby they nonetheless racked up thirty-four tries and finished the group with a plus 208 points record. In the quarter-finals they were drawn against old foes Wales. This was to be an altogether different encounter and the inspired Welsh went into the break with a 10-3 lead. England however rallied and a magnificent run from deep inside, allowing Robinson to send Greenwood over for a try that levelled the scores. From there England built a lead, eventually running out 28-17 winners.

France lay in wait at the semi-final stage and although England were unable to land a try, four dropped goals and six penalties from Wilkinson's boot meant that the outcome was never in doubt.

Only world champions Australia, who England had beaten four times in as many years, now remained. This time they would face them in a World Cup Final in Sydney in front of a partisan crowd of 83,000. Undaunted the English pack took control in the first-half allowing Wilkinson to cancel out an early Australian try, before Robinson burned through the home defence to give England a 14-5 lead at the break. Indiscipline then allowed the Aussies back into the game and a last-minute penalty allowed them to level the scores at 17-17, before the end of normal time.

Extra time followed with neither side able to break the deadlock. Jason Leonard, veteran of 1991, came on and the flow of penalties to Australia evaporated. Then with seconds remaining another substitute, Moody, won a line-out so that Dawson and Johnson could zig-zag their way towards the Australian line. With no time left on the clock Wilkinson landed the winning dropped goal. Moments later Catt cleared to touch, Greenwood embraced Wilkinson and England had won the 2003 Rugby World Cup in the most dramatic of circumstances.

Several key members of the side, including captain Martin Johnson, retired immediately after the tournament but did so in the knowledge that they helped bring about the single greatest sporting achievement in the history of English rugby. The class of 2003 had conquered all before them and won all there was to win.

Left: Leonard and Dawson on flight home, 2003.

Below: Clive Woodward's inspiring message to England fans, 2003.

You're a champion, too. We are all part of 'One Team' — that is why the World Cup is where it belongs. Clive — Xmas 03

15

Full-back

LENNARD STOKES (1875-1881)
Birthplace: Greenwich
Position: Wing, Three-quarter, Full-back
Total Caps: 12
Calcutta Cups: 2 (+1 retained)
Triple Crowns: n/a
Outright Championship Victories: n/a
Grand Slams: n/a
World Cups: n/a

While Len Stokes' older brother Fred was England's first captain, Len might lay claim to having been English rugby's first star player.

A safe and brilliant tackler, he was chiefly regarded for his pace, dodging powers, clever feet and 'capital knowledge of the science of the game'. He was also technically gifted, described as having 'the longest and surest drop-kick in the kingdom' in the late 1870s. All of this, he put to good use as either a wing or full-back with license to roam.

His international debut coincided with Ireland's introduction to international rugby and he helped England to defeat them in his first game in 1875. The following year his conversion helped England to the Calcutta Cup and a clean sweep of victories.

In 1880 Stokes was instated as captain and England secured another clean sweep. His final game came against Scotland in 1881. He had earned twelve caps, including five as captain. His seventeen international career conversions remained an English record for over 100 years.

HERBERT 'OCTOPUS' TREMLETT GAMLIN
(1899-1904)
Birthplace: West Buckland
Position: Full-back
Total Caps: 15
Calcutta Cups: 1
Triple Crowns: 0
Outright Championship Victories: 0
Grand Slams: n/a
World Cups: n/a

At a time when a player's England career was fleeting and brief, Octopus Gamlin was ever present for five consecutive seasons between 1899 and 1904. These were years of struggle for England and Gamlin was called into defensive duties in most of the games in which he played. But it was defensively that Gamlin excelled, time and again he served his country magnificently as their last-line-of defence and put in a man of the match performance when winning the Calcutta Cup in 1902.

Beautifully described by venerable rugby historian John Griffiths as 'a beacon in a stormy sea, against the waves of sweeping Welsh three-quarter movements,' Gamlin earned the nickname 'Octopus' on account of his ability to stop opposition players, frequently tackling two men at once with two (or more) arms.

HAROLD 'TUPPY' GEOFFREY OWEN
OWEN-SMITH (1934-1937)
Birthplace: Rondebosch
Position: Full-Back
Total Caps: 10
Calcutta Cups: 4
Triple Crowns: 3
Outright Championship Victories: 2
Grand Slams: n/a
World Cups: n/a

England's last line of defence throughout much of the 1930s was a scar-faced champion lightweight boxer called Tuppy Owen-Smith. As befitting a former boxer Owen-Smith, though wiry of frame, was tough as old boots and an all-round rugby player with terrific pace and a fiercely combative spirit that often saw him spear-head attacks from the rear.

Born in Cape Town, Owen-Smith had played five cricket test matches for South Africa in 1929. He was selected for the English rugby team in 1934 and immediately helped his side to a clean sweep of victories, outright championship win and Triple Crown in his fill first season.

Left out of the 1935 side he returned in 1936 to help England to their first ever victory against New Zealand. The following season Owen-Smith was instated as captain and ended his international career by leading his side to another clean sweep, outright championship win and Triple Crown.

A popular and humorous figure on and off the pitch, Owen-Smith trained as a physician and returned to South Africa before serving in the Middle East during the Second World War. He earned ten caps in total.

ROBERT HILLER (1968-1972)
Birthplace: Woking
Position: Full-back
Total Caps: 19
Calcutta Cups: 2
Triple Crowns: 0
Outright Championship Victories: 0
Grand Slams: 0
World Cups: n/a

Bob Hiller was a natural leader on the field and in 1969 became only the third full-back to be given the England captaincy. His position was not deemed to be an impediment, 'with everyone in front you can see exactly what is happening' he explained.

Away from the field Hiller was a hard taskmaster who attempted to instil a winning mentality through rigid training and positive thinking.

Hiller was one of the last proponents of the punted place-kick, preferring to kick his side's penalties and conversions with his big toe rather than his instep. At this he excelled; the 138 points that he had landed by the time of his final cap in 1972 was a then English record.

He kicked England to a Calcutta Cup victory at Murrayfield during his first full international season and led England to a first ever victory over the Springboks, at Twickenham in 1969.

In all he amassed nineteen caps and described leading the national side as 'the greatest honour that has ever come my way'.

ALISTAIR JAMES HIGNELL (1975-1979)
Birthplace: Ely
Position: Full-back
Total Caps: 14
Calcutta Cups: 1 (+1 retained)
Triple Crowns: 0
Outright Championship Victories: 0
Grand Slams: 0
World Cups: n/a

The Cricket Society voted Alistair Hignell the 'most promising young cricketer of the year' in 1974. He did go on to score seven centuries for Gloucestershire but it was in rugby union that he achieved national representative honours.

Initially a scrum-half, Hignell was switched to full-back while still a student and his speed, handling and ability to read the game brought him immediate success.

He was first selected for England during their 1975 tour of Australia. The following year he made his home debut, kicking eleven of England's twenty-three points in a victory against the Wallabies. Over five seasons he kicked a total of forty-eight points in fourteen appearances and regularly earned plaudits for his marshalling of defence during difficult years for the national side.

Upon retirement Hignell was briefly a teacher before taking up commentary, covering each of the first six Rugby World Cup tournaments. In 1999 Hignell was diagnosed with multiple sclerosis but continued behind the mic until 2008. His final game was the Premiership final between Leicester and Wasps, which match-winning captain Lawrence Dallaglio dedicated to the much-loved commentator.

Drawing on the reserves that typified his career as a sportsman Hignell describes his experiences with MS as transformative:

> I feel blessed to have MS, which seems a funny thing to say about a disabling progressive and incurable disease. But it has sent me on a journey I would never have had otherwise, and I think that it has enabled me to find out how good, loving and generous people are in general.

WILLIAM 'DUSTY' HENRY HARE (1974-1984)
Birthplace: West Buckland
Position: Full-back
Total Caps: 25
Calcutta Cups: 2
Triple Crowns: 1
Outright Championship Victories: 1
Grand Slams: 1
World Cups: n/a

Full-back Dusty Hare's England career spanned for over a decade. He earned his first cap in 1974 but had to wait until 1978 for his second. During that time he added the art of nerveless place-kicking to his repertoire of running skills. In 1979 he became England's first choice full-back and would go on to feature in every round of England's Grand Slam-winning year of 1980.

Hare landed eight penalties and five conversions during the 1980 championship including three at Twickenham against Wales. The last of these came from a tight angle, in stoppage time, with England trailing 6-8. The game had been wrought with extreme tension but Hare remained impressively calm and won the game for England.

By the end of his career Hare had scored 240 points in twenty-five international matches. At club level he had amassed over 7,000. Throughout his career and for many years after Hare worked as a full-time farmer in his native Nottinghamshire.

JONATHAN MARK WEBB (1987-1993)
Birthplace: Ealing
Position: Full-back
Total Caps: 33
Calcutta Cups: 3 (+1 retained)
Triple Crowns: 1
Outright Championship Victories: 1
Grand Slams: 1
World Cups: Finalist

Jon Webb was always clear that his main aim in rugby was to enjoy himself. But his apparently laid-back attitude didn't prevent him from racking up the accolades and he retired from international rugby having scored more points for England than any other player.

A surgeon by profession, his quietly spoken manner off the field was complemented by a fluent and graceful playing style on it. Unyielding in defence, he was confident under the high-balls and dangerous in attack.

He made his debut for England as a substitute against Australia in England's first ever World Cup game. He lost his place in 1989 but won it back in time for the 1991 World Cup where he helped steer England to the final. There he kicked England's only points of the match.

The following season he was a standout performer, scoring three tries and a record sixty-seven points in helping England to secure a second consecutive Grand Slam. He retired in 1993 with thirty-three caps and 296 points.

MATTHEW BRENDAN PERRY (1997-2001)
Birthplace: Bath
Position: Full-back
Total Caps: 36
Calcutta Cups: 1
Triple Crowns: 1
Outright Championship Victories: 2
Grand Slams: 0
World Cups: Quarter-finalist

In 1997 Matt Perry became the third generation of his family to represent Bath and made his international debut shortly afterwards at the age of twenty. A fast, adventurous back, he played centre as well as full-back and was immediately welcomed by England fans for his preference for running from deep with the ball in hand.

A try against Ireland helped his side to the Triple Crown in 1998 and the following year Perry played in the quarter-finals of the 1999 Rugby World Cup.

He would secure outright championship victories in 2000 and 2001 as part of a rapidly improving England side and at the age of twenty-three became England's most capped full-back of all time.

Though serious injuries would prevent him from significantly adding to his total, Perry nonetheless played his last game for England in 2001, having amassed thirty-six caps that included ten tries and fifty points.

OWEN JOSHUA LEWSEY (1998-2007)
Birthplace: Bromley
Position: Full-back
Total Caps: 55
Calcutta Cups: 3
Triple Crowns: 1
Outright Championship Victories: 1
Grand Slams: 1
World Cups: 1

Josh Lewsey exuded attacking guile and solid defence and had the versatility and intelligence to play as a wing, centre, fly-half or full-back.

He was also possessed of a fierce competitiveness and made enough waves to be selected for the England southern hemisphere tour of 1998 at the age of twenty-one. The tour however was not a success and Lewsey found himself back in the wilderness after just three caps.

But Lewsey was not the sort to sit around feeling sorry for himself. It took him three years to return to the international fold, during which time he had completed a year's training as an army lieutenant at Sandhurst.

'You learn far more out of failure than you do out of success'

He was reselected in 2001 and scored three tries in four games as England toured North America. Having found a way back into the squad he then exploded into the first XV during the 2003 6 Nations, scoring three tries on the way to a Grand Slam.

After helping England to back-to-back away wins against New Zealand and Australia he then landed five tries against Uruguay in the group stages of the 2003 World Cup. Three weeks later he helped England become world champions.

He contributed tries in 2004 and 2005 before being one of England's standout performers in the 2007 World Cup campaign, scoring a try in the semi-final win against France, before succumbing to injury.

The semi-final would be the last of his fifty-five caps, in which he scored twenty-two tries.

JASON ROBINSON (2001-2007)
Birthplace: Leeds
Position: Full-back
Total Caps: 51
Calcutta Cups: 5
Triple Crowns: 2
Outright Championship Victories: 2
Grand Slams: 1
World Cups: 1

A full-back has two principle methods of attack; he can run or he can kick. Jason Robinson never kicked. It wasn't that he couldn't, he could, but such was his acceleration, footwork and vision that he would almost always carry the ball further. A master of the elusive run he admitted after he retired that he had generally beaten the first man in his head before he had even reached him.

A Rugby League convert, Robinson had reached a Rugby League World Cup Final in 1995 before switching codes. Some union coaches tried to temper his penchant to roam, but Robinson's attacking spirit was not to be tempered.

'Only dead fish go with the flow' were his words when describing how a transformational period in his life had seen him, as a born-again Christian, swap Saturday nightclubbing with serving the homeless from inside a Manchester soup kitchen.

Robinson didn't so much convert to Rugby Union as Rugby Union converted to him. Within weeks he had been selected for England and then the 2001 British and Irish Lions.

After switching from wing to full-back, he scored eight tries in six matches during the 2001/02 season, adding a Triple Crown to the 6 Nations title of 2001.

In 2003 his brace against Scotland set England on their way to a first Grand Slam in eight seasons. Later that year he was a key player in England's run to the final of the 2003 Rugby World Cup and his sensational try against Australia in the final put England in control of a match that would deliver the Webb Ellis Cup for the first time.

In 2004 he earned the first of seven caps as captain before retiring from international rugby in 2005. Two years later he returned to the side, scoring four tries in the 2007 6 Nations Championship and spearheading another run to the final of the 2007 Rugby World Cup.

His final international performance ended in narrow defeat but Robinson came out of retirement to help the Barbarians defeat the world champions later that year.

Robinson, nicknamed 'Billy Whizz', scored twenty-eight tries in fifty-one appearances.

Roll of Honour

1 John Bentley
2 Reginald Birkett
3 Benjamin Burns
4 John Clayton
5 Charles Arthur Crompton
6 Alfred Davenport
7 John Dugdale
8 Arthur Gibson
9 Joseph Green
10 Arthur Guillemard
11 Alfred St. George Hamersley
12 John Luscombe
13 Arthur Lyon
14 William MacLaren
15 Richard Osborne
16 Charles Sherrard
17 Frederick Stokes
18 Frank Tobin
19 Dawson Turner
20 H. J. C. Turner
21 Thomas Batson
22 James Body
23 James Bush
24 Frederick Currey
25 Francis d'Aguilar
26 Stephen Finney
27 Harold Freeman
28 Francis Isherwood
29 Francis Luscombe
30 James Mackinlay
31 Frederick Mills
32 William Moberly
33 Nipper Pinching
34 P. Wilkinson

35 Cecil Boyle
36 Ernest Cheston
37 William Fletcher
38 Henry Arnold Lawrence
39 Henry Marsh
40 Murray Marshall
41 Sydney Morse
42 Cyril Rickards
43 Ernest Still
44 Charles Vanderspar
45 John Batten
46 Marshall Brooks
47 Henry Bryden
48 William Collins
49 Charles Crosse
50 Foster Cunliffe
51 Jacob Genth
52 Edward Kewley
53 William Milton
54 Sydney Parker
55 William Stafford
56 Roger Walker
57 Frank Adams
58 Edward Fraser
59 Harry Graham
60 William Hutchinson
61 Arthur Michell
62 Edward Nash
63 Alec Pearson
64 Edward Perrott
65 Lennard Stokes
66 Louis Birkett
67 Wyndham Evanson
68 Josiah Edward Paul

69 Jeaffreson Vennor Brewer
70 Charles Bryden
71 Andrew Bulteel
72 Charles Clark
73 John Graham
74 Walter Greg
75 Charles Gunner
76 Spencer Login
77 Ernest Marriott
78 Edward Beadon Turner
79 Courteney Verelst
80 Arthur Heath
81 William Hunt
82 William Hutchinson
83 Frederic Lee
84 William Rawlinson
85 Thomas Tetley
86 George Turner
87 Henry Fowler
88 Gilbert Harrison
89 Monkey Hornby
90 P. L. A. Price
91 Charles Touzel
92 Harry Garnett
93 Archibald Law
94 Robert Todd
95 John Biggs
96 Frank Fowler
97 Howard Fowler
98 Temple Gurdon
99 Henry Kayll
100 George Thomson
101 George Vernon
102 John Bell

103 Thomas Blatherwick
104 Jimmy Budd
105 Ernest Dawson
106 Henry Enthoven
107 Herbert Gardner
108 Allan Jackson
109 William Penny
110 George Burton
111 Henry Huth
112 Norman McLeod
113 Stuart Neame
114 Hugh Rowley
115 Henry Springmann
116 Henry Taylor
117 Harold Bateson
118 William Openshaw
119 Henry Twynam
120 Sidney Ellis
121 Thomas Fry
122 Charles Gurdon
123 Robert Hunt
124 Barron Kilner
125 Ellis Markendale
126 John Schofield
127 Ernest Woodhead
128 Charles Coates
129 Richard Finch
130 Charles Phillips
131 Charles Sawyer
132 Charles Fernandes
133 Walter Hewitt
134 John Ravenscroft
135 Ryder Richardson
136 James Ward
137 Harry Vassall
138 Charles Plumpton Wilson
139 Frank Wright
140 Edmund Beswick
141 Wilfred Bolton
142 Herbert Fuller
143 James Hunt
144 Bernard Middleton
145 Aubrey Spurling
146 Philip Newton
147 John Payne
148 William Tatham
149 Arthur Evanson
150 Robert Henderson
151 Richard Kindersley
152 Alan Rotherham
153 G. Standing
154 Arthur Taylor
155 Charles Wade
156 Charles Wooldridge
157 Edward Moore
158 Richard Pattisson
159 Henry Tristram
160 Charles Chapman
161 Charles Marriott
162 Edward Strong
163 Henry Bell
164 Herbert Fallas
165 Charles Sample
166 Alfred Teggin
167 Henry Wigglesworth
168 Albert Wood
169 Edward Court
170 John Hawcridge
171 Arthur Kemble
172 F. Moss
173 Henry Ryalls
174 Andrew Stoddart
175 Charles Horley
176 Fred Bonsor
177 William Clibbon
178 Charles Elliot
179 Froude Hancock
180 Rupert Inglis
181 George Jeffery
182 Rawson Robertshaw
183 Edgar Wilkinson
184 Norman Spurling
185 Ernest Brutton
186 Hiatt Baker
187 Charles Cleveland
188 John Dewhurst
189 John Hickson
190 John le Fleming
191 Richard 'Dicky' Lockwood
192 Sam Roberts
193 Robert Seddon
194 Arthur Fagan
195 Frank Pease
196 Mason Scott
197 Charles Anderton
198 Harry Bedford
199 John Cave
200 Frank Evershed
201 Donald Jowett
202 Frederick Lowrie
203 Arthur Robinson
204 Arthur Royle
205 William Martin Scott
206 John Sutcliffe
207 Harry Wilkinson
208 William Yiend
209 Richard Budworth
210 Francis Hugh Fox
211 William Grant Mitchell
212 Piercy Morrison
213 John Rogers
214 James Valentine
215 Sammy Woods
216 James Wright
217 Randolph Aston
218 John Dyson
219 Edgar Holmes
220 John Toothill
221 William Spence
222 Frederic Alderson
223 John Berry
224 William Bromet
225 Percy Christopherson
226 Tom Kent
227 William Leake
228 Eustace North
229 Joseph Richards
230 Roger Wilson
231 Launcelot Percival
232 Edgar Bonham-Carter
233 Alfred Allport
234 Arthur Briggs
235 Edward Bullough

236 Charles Emmott
237 George Hubbard
238 William Nicholl
239 James Pyke
240 W. B. Thomson
241 Abel Ashworth
242 Samuel Houghton
243 James Marsh
244 Ernest Taylor
245 Harry Bradshaw
246 Thomas Coop
247 Harry Varley
248 Tom Broadley
249 Robert de Winton
250 Edwin Field
251 John Greenwell
252 Frederick Lohden
253 Howard Marshall
254 Philip Maud
255 Horace Duckett
256 Thomas Nicholson
257 Frederic Jones
258 John Robinson
259 Buster Soane
260 Cyril Wells
261 Fred Byrne
262 Frederick Firth
263 John Hall
264 Charles Hooper
265 Samuel Morfitt
266 Harry Speed
267 William Eldon
    Tucker
268 Robert Wood
269 Albert Elliott
270 Walter Jesse
    Jackson
271 William Walton
272 Edward Baker
273 Godfrey Carey
274 Richard Cattell
275 John Fegan
276 Horace William
    Finlinson
277 Frederick Leslie-
    Jones
278 Frank Mitchell
279 Francis Poole

280 Charles Thomas
281 Herbert Ward
282 Thomas Dobson
283 Ernest Fookes
284 Lyndhurst Giblin
285 John Pinch
286 John Rhodes
287 Anthony Starks
288 John William Ward
289 W. Bobby Whiteley
290 James Baron
291 George Hughes
292 Edward Knowles
293 Bob Poole
294 William Ashford
295 Francis Byrne
296 Percy Ebdon
297 Thomas 'Tom'
    Fletcher
298 Frederick Jacob
299 Roland Mangles
300 Robert Oakes
301 Wilfred Stoddart
302 Frank Stout
303 William Bunting
304 Samuel Northmore
305 Tot Robinson
306 John Taylor
307 James Davidson
308 Herbert Dudgeon
309 Osbert Mackie
310 Joseph Blacklock
311 Philip Jacob
312 Harry Myers
313 Richard Pierce
314 Frederick Shaw
315 Charles Edward
    Wilson
316 William Pilkington
317 Harold Ramsden
318 Arthur Rotherham
319 Percy Royds
320 James Shaw
321 Percy Stout
322 Geoffrey Unwin
323 Robert Livesay
324 John Daniell
325 Joseph Davidson

326 Reginald Forrest
327 Octopus Gamlin
328 George Ralph
    Gibson
329 Charles Harper
330 William Mortimer
331 Stanley Anderson
332 Arthur Darby
333 John Shooter
334 Aubrey Dowson
335 Reginald Hobbs
336 John Matters
337 Reginald Schwarz
338 Bim Baxter
339 Fred Bell
340 Robert William
    Bell
341 Arthur Brettargh
342 William Cobby
343 Arthur Cockerham
344 Sydney Coopper
345 Gerald Gordon-
    Smith
346 Wallace Jarman
347 George Marsden
348 Elliot Nicholson
349 Shirley Reynolds
350 Charles Scott
351 Harry Alexander
352 John Marquis
353 Alexander Todd
354 Arthur Luxmoore
355 Edgar Elliot
356 Nigel Fletcher
357 Charles Gibson
358 David Graham
359 Arthur O'Neill
360 Ernest Roberts
361 John Sagar
362 Whacker Smith
363 Elliott Vivyan
364 Katie Walton
365 Colin Hall
366 Robert Wood
367 Norman Cox
368 Charles Edgar
369 Bernard Charles
    Hartley

370 Toggie Kendall
371 Bernard Oughtred
372 Henry Weston
373 Denys Dobson
374 George Fraser
375 John Jewitt
376 Philip Nicholas
377 John Raphael
378 Leonard Tosswill
379 T. J. Willcocks
380 Samuel Williams
381 Peter Hardwick
382 Thomas Simpson
383 Robert Bradley
384 Vincent Cartwright
385 James Duthie
386 Frankie Hulme
387 Jack Miles
388 Reginald Spooner
389 Walter Heppel
390 Basil Hill
391 Edward Barrett
392 Walter Butcher
393 Edward Dillon
394 Patrick Hancock
395 George Keeton
396 Jumbo Milton
397 Norman Moore
398 Charles Joseph
    Newbold
399 William Cave
400 Thomas Gibson
401 Samuel Irvin
402 John Mathias
403 Francis Palmer
404 Walter Rogers
405 John Green
406 William Grylls
407 Harry Shewring
408 Chris Stanger-
    Leathes
409 George Vickery
410 Curly Hammond
411 Sidney Osborne
412 Adrian Stoop
413 Jacky Braithwaite
414 Dai Gent
415 Reginald Godfray

416 Alfred Hind
417 Henry Imrie
418 John Jackett
419 Richard Russell
420 George
    Summerscale
421 George Dobbs
422 Harold Hodges
423 Arthur Hudson
424 Raphael Jago
425 Thomas Kelly
426 Alf Kewney
427 William Mills
428 James Hutchinson
429 Cecil Milton
430 Joseph Sandford
431 John Birkett
432 Robert Dibble
433 James Peters
434 Cecil Shaw
435 Thomas Hogarth
436 Arnold Alcock
437 Freddie Brooks
438 Tremlett Batchelor
439 John Hopley
440 Daniel Lambert
441 Harry Lee
442 William Nanson
443 Andrew Slocock
444 Thomas Wedge
445 Frank Scott
446 Jumbo Leather
447 Arthur Pickering
448 Walter Wilson
449 Andrew Newton
450 Khaki Roberts
451 Sydney Start
452 Patsy Boylan
453 Ernest Chambers
454 Harold Havelock
455 Walter Lapage
456 Garnet Portus
457 Herbert Sibree
458 Alf Wood
459 R. Gilbert
460 Rupert
    Williamson
461 Henry Vassall

462 Fischer Burges-
    Watson
463 Maffer Davey
464 George Lyon
465 William Oldham
466 Tommy Woods
467 Alec Ashcroft
468 Eric Assinder
469 Barrie Bennetts
470 John Cooper
471 Percy Down
472 Frederick Knight
473 Edgar Mobbs
474 Alfred Morris
475 Sid Penny
476 Frank Tarr
477 Herbert Archer
478 Frank Handford
479 Ernest Ibbitson
480 William Johns
481 Charles Bolton
482 Frank Hutchinson
483 Ronald Poulton-
    Palmer
484 Harold Morton
485 Alexander Palmer
486 Arthur Wilson
487 Cyril Wright
488 Harold Harrison
489 Lancelot
    Barrington-Ward
490 Harry Berry
491 Fred Chapman
492 Leonard Haigh
493 William Johnston
494 Cherry Pillman
495 Fenton Smith
496 Barney Solomon
497 Leslie Hayward
498 Alan Adams
499 Harry Coverdale
500 Reginald Hands
501 Anthony Henniker-
    Gotley
502 John Ritson
503 Edward
    Scorfield
504 Cyril Williams

505 Norman Wodehouse
506 Guy Hind
507 Percy Lawrie
508 Tim Stoop
509 Bruno Brown
510 John King
511 William Mann
512 Alan Roberts
513 John Scholfield
514 Stanley Williams
515 Ronald Lagden
516 Henry Brougham
517 John Eddison
518 Dave Holland
519 Alfred MacIlwaine
520 John Pym
521 Dick Stafford
522 Jenny Greenwood
523 William Hynes
524 Maurice Neale
525 William Cheesman
526 Vincent Coates
527 Dave Davies
528 Cyril Lowe
529 Sidney Smart
530 Francis Steinthal
531 George Ward
532 Arthur Dingle
533 Alfred Kitching
534 Francis Oakeley
535 Joseph Brunton
536 Arthur Bull
537 Alfred Maynard
538 Tim Taylor
539 Bungy Watson
540 Pedlar Wood
541 Arthur Harrison
542 Robert Pillman
543 Francis Stone
544 Alexander Sykes
545 Barry Cumberlege
546 Harold Day
547 Ernest Hammett
548 George Holford
549 Cecil Kershaw
550 Jannie Krige
551 Frank Mellish

552 Laurence Merriam
553 James Morgan
554 Wavell Wakefield
555 Jock Wright
556 Geoffrey Conway
557 Wilfrid Lowry
558 Harry Millett
559 Alastair Smallwood
560 Frank Taylor
561 Stan Harris
562 Edward Myers
563 Tom Voyce
564 Arthur Blakiston
565 Tom Woods
566 Reg Edwards
567 Ernest Gardner
568 Ronald Cove-Smith
569 Quentin King
570 Leonard Corbett
571 Vivian Davies
572 Sam Tucker
573 Matthew Bradby
574 Robert Duncan
575 John Maxwell-Hyslop
576 Reginald Pickles
577 Leo Price
578 John Middleton
579 James Pitman
580 Peveril William-Powlett
581 Frederick Gilbert
582 William Luddington
583 Frank Sanders
584 Toff Holliday
585 Harold Locke
586 Carston Catcheside
587 Bevan Chantrill
588 Jake Jacob
589 Alan Robson
590 Arthur Young
591 Chubby Faithfull
592 Richard Hamilton-Wickes
593 Jim Brough
594 John Gibbs
595 Ronald Hillard

596 Harold Kittermaster
597 Rex Armstrong
598 Edward Massey
599 Joe Periton
600 Richard Lawson
601 Roderick MacLennan
602 Duncan Cumming
603 Stanley Considine
604 Alfred Aslett
605 Hyde Burton
606 Tom Francis
607 Bob Hanvey
608 Edward Stanbury
609 John Worton
610 Thomas Devitt
611 Leslie Haslett
612 Bill Tucker
613 James Webb
614 Thomas Coulson
615 Jerry Hanley
616 Colin Laird
617 Monkey Sellar
618 Kendrick Stark
619 Harry Davies
620 Wallace Eyres
621 Douglas Law
622 William Pratten
623 William Alexander
624 Colin Bishop
625 Ralph Buckingham
626 Jack Wallens
627 Carl Aarvold
628 William Kirwan-Taylor
629 Thomas Lawson
630 James Richardson
631 David Turquand-Young
632 Godfrey Palmer
633 Doug Prentice
634 Robert Sparks
635 Thomas Brown
636 Robert Foulds
637 Geoffrey Sladen
638 Robert Smeddle
639 John Swayne

640 Herbert Whitley
641 Harry Wilkinson
642 Guy Wilson
643 Thomas Harris
644 Stephen Meikle
645 Tony Novis
646 Henry Rew
647 Edward Richards
648 Eric Coley
649 Charles Gummer
650 Sam Martindale
651 Jim Reeve
652 Roger Spong
653 John Askew
654 Alfred Bateson
655 Brian Black
656 Jeff Forrest
657 Peter Howard
658 Joe Kendrew
659 Frank Malir
660 Matthew Robson
661 Wilf Sobey
662 Alan Key
663 Peter Brook
664 John Hubbard
665 Christopher Tanner
666 Jimmy Barrington
667 Lawrence Bedford
668 Maurice
    Bonaventura
669 Donald Burland
670 Richard Davey
671 Maurice McCanlis
672 Brian Pope
673 Deneys Swayne
674 Tinny Dean
675 Pop Dunkley
676 Gordon Gregory
677 Ernest Harding
678 Cliff Harrison
679 Peter Hordorn
680 Tom Knowles
681 John Tallent
682 Eric Whiteley
683 Bobby Barr
684 Alfred Carpenter
685 Ronald Gerrard
686 Reginald Hobbs

687 John Hodgson
688 Doug Norman
689 Arthur Rowley
690 Leslie Saxby
691 Charles Webb
692 Barney Evans
693 Walter Elliot
694 Bernard Gadney
695 Reginald Roberts
696 Arthur Vaughan-
    Jones
697 Ray Longland
698 Reginald Bolton
699 Lewis Booth
700 Anthony
    Roncoroni
701 Edward Harry
    Sadler
702 Carlton Troop
703 William Weston
704 Peter Cranmer
705 John Dicks
706 Henry Fry
707 Graham Meikle
708 Tuppy Owen-Smith
709 Tim Warr
710 John Wright
711 Charles Slow
712 Harold Boughton
713 Peter Candler
714 Allan Clarke
715 Arthur Cridlan
716 Jimmy Giles
717 Jack Heaton
718 Dudley Kemp
719 Bus Leyland
720 Ernie Nicholson
721 Arthur Payne
722 Dick Auty
723 Edward Hamilton-
    Hill
724 Alexander
    Obolensky
725 Hal Sever
726 Harold Wheatley
727 Herbert Toft
728 Arthur Butler
729 David Campbell

730 Thomas Huskisson
731 Tommy Kemp
732 Dermot Milman
733 Robin Prescott
734 Arthur Wheatley
735 John Cook
736 Jeff Reynolds
737 Jimmy Unwin
738 Trilby Freakes
739 Basil Nicholson
740 Robert Marshall
741 Grahame Parker
742 Alan Brown
743 Tom Berry
744 Robert Carr
745 Paul Cooke
746 Dickie Guest
747 George Hancock
748 Derek Teden
749 Gus Walker
750 John Watkins
751 Jack Ellis
752 Ernest Parsons
753 Billy Bennett
754 Arthur Gray
755 Nim Hall
756 Alan Henderson
757 Geoffrey Kelly
758 Bill Moore
759 Joe Mycock
760 Samuel Perry
761 Edward Scott
762 Micky Steele-
    Bodger
763 David Swarbrick
764 Jika Travers
765 Harry Walker
766 Don White
767 Squib Donnelly
768 James George
769 Cyril Holmes
770 Ossie Newton-
    Thompson
771 Bob Weighill
772 George Gibbs
773 Syd Newman
774 Vic Roberts
775 Eric Evans

776 John Keeling
777 Richard Madge
778 Douglas Vaughan
779 Humphrey Luya
780 Ivor Preece
781 Dick Uren
782 Thomas Price
783 Martin Turner
784 Lewis Cannell
785 Patrick Sykes
786 Allan Towell
787 Mike Berridge
788 Bryan Braithwaite-
     Exley
789 Thompson Danby
790 Jack Gregory
791 Barry Holmes
792 Edward Horsfall
793 Geoffrey Hosking
794 Gordon Rimmer
795 Clive van Ryneveld
796 John Kendall-
     Carpenter
797 Robert Kennedy
798 John Matthews
799 John Steeds
800 Brian Boobbyer
801 Ian Botting
802 John Cain
803 Murray Hofmeyer
804 Wally Holmes
805 Herbert Jones
806 Harry Small
807 John Smith
808 Stanley John
     Adkins
809 John Hyde
810 John Baume
811 Jasper Bartlett
812 Edwin Hewitt
813 Philip Moore
814 Lionel Oakley
815 George Rittson-
     Thomas
816 Trevor Smith
817 Bob Stirling
818 Victor Tindall
819 Squire Wilkins

820 Peter Woodruff
821 Evan Hardy
822 Bruce Neale
823 John Williams
824 William Hook
825 Dennis
     Shuttleworth
826 Albert Agar
827 Alec Lewis
828 Chris Winn
829 Ted Woodward
830 Elliott Woodgate
831 Philip Collins
832 Reginald Bazley
833 Nick Labuschagne
834 Martin Regan
835 Jeff Butterfield
836 Dyson Stayt Wilson
837 Phil Davies
838 Reg Higgins
839 Ian King
840 Pat Quinn
841 Sandy Sanders
842 Peter Yarranton
843 Peter Young
844 John Bance
845 Nigel Gibbs
846 Vic Leadbetter
847 Ernie Robinson
848 Johnny Williams
849 Doug Baker
850 William Hancock
851 George Hastings
852 David Hazell
853 Peter Ryan
854 Philip Joseph
     Taylor
855 Ian Beer
856 Harry Scott
857 Frank Sykes
858 Noel Estcourt
859 Fenwick Allison
860 Ned Ashcroft
861 John Currie
862 Peter Jackson
863 Ron Jacobs
864 Dickie Jeeps
865 David Marques

866 Peter Robbins
867 Mike Smith
868 Peter Thompson
869 Ricky Bartlett
870 Bob Challis
871 Philip Horrocks-
     Taylor
872 Ronald Syrett
873 Jim Hetherington
874 Malcolm Phillips
875 John Young
876 Alfred Herbert
877 John Scott
878 Gordon Bendon
879 Bev Risman
880 Stephen Smith
881 John Wackett
882 Larry Webb
883 Brian Wightman
884 Jeff Clements
885 Herbert Godwin
886 Stanley Hodgson
887 William Morgan
888 James Roberts
889 Don Rutherford
890 Richard Sharp
891 Mike Weston
892 Peter Wright
893 Bill Patterson
894 Laurance Rimmer
895 Ray French
896 Mike Gavins
897 John Price
898 Budge Rogers
899 John Willcox
900 Victor Harding
901 Phil Judd
902 Adrian Underwood
903 Michael Wade
904 John Dee
905 Andrew Hurst
906 Thomas Pargetter
907 Stanley Purdy
908 Simon Clarke
909 Mike Davis
910 Beverley Dovey
911 Nick Drake-Lee
912 Dick Manley

913 John Owen
914 John Thorne
915 David Perry
916 Tug Wilson
917 Roger Hosen
918 Victor Marriott
919 John Ranson
920 Roger Sangwin
921 Peter Ford
922 Bob Rowell
923 Thomas Brophy
924 Colin Payne
925 Tony Peart
926 Frederick Wrench
927 Geoffrey
       Frankcom
928 Tony Horton
929 Stephen Richards
930 David Rosser
931 Ted Rudd
932 Nicholas Silk
933 Colin Simpson
934 Peter Cook
935 Andy Hancock
936 Terence Arthur
937 David Powell
938 John Pullin
939 Keith Savage
940 Jeremy Spencer
941 Bob Taylor
942 Clive Ashby
943 Dick Greenwood
944 Colin McFadyean
945 William Treadwell
946 Bob Hearn
947 George Sherriff
948 Trevor Wintle
949 Mike Coulman
950 Peter Glover
951 Christopher
       Jennins
952 Peter Larter
953 John Barton
954 John Finlan
955 John Pallant
956 Roger Pickering
957 Dave Rollitt
958 David Watt

959 Rodney Webb
960 William Gittings
961 Bob Lloyd
962 Peter Bell
963 David Gay
964 Bob Hiller
965 Brian Keen
966 Jim Parsons
967 Derek Prout
968 Bill Redwood
969 Bryan West
970 Terence Brooke
971 David Duckham
972 Keith Fairbrother
973 Keith Fielding
974 Nigel Horton
975 John Spencer
976 Timothy Dalton
977 Kenneth Plummer
978 Tony Bucknall
979 Martin Hale
980 Ian Shackleton
981 Nigel Starmer-
       Smith
982 Brian 'Stack'
       Stevens
983 Christopher
       Wardlow
984 Michael Novak
985 Mike Bulpitt
986 Barry Jackson
987 Tony Jorden
988 Mike Leadbetter
989 Gerald Redmond
990 Ronald Hannaford
991 Jeremy Janion
992 Tony Neary
993 Barry Ninnes
994 Jacko Page
995 Peter Rossborough
996 Ian Wright
997 Fran Cotton
998 Dick Cowman
999 Chris Ralston
1000 Roger Creed
1001 Peter Dixon
1002 Michael Beese
1003 Alan Brinn

1004 Mike Burton
1005 Alan Old
1006 Andy Ripley
1007 Jan Webster
1008 Peter Knight
1009 Lionel Weston
1010 Nicholas Martin
1011 Geoff Evans
1012 Sam Doble
1013 Alan Morley
1014 Peter Preece
1015 John Watkins
1016 William Anderson
1017 Peter Warfield
1018 Steve Smith
1019 Roger Uttley
1020 Martin Cooper
1021 Peter Squires
1022 David Roughley
1023 Keith Smith
1024 Dusty Hare
1025 Bill Beaumont
1026 Peter Wheeler
1027 Neil Bennett
1028 Peter Butler
1029 Peter Kingston
1030 Neil Mantell
1031 Andy Maxwell
1032 Barry Nelmes
1033 Alan Wordsworth
1034 Alastair Hignell
1035 Bob Wilkinson
1036 Barry Corless
1037 Mark Keyworth
1038 Mike Lampkowski
1039 David Cooke
1040 Derek Wyatt
1041 Garry Adey
1042 Mike Slemen
1043 Christopher
       Williams
1044 Robin Cowling
1045 Charles Kent
1046 Mike Rafter
1047 Malcolm Young
1048 John Scott
1049 Paul Dodge
1050 John Horton

1051 Bob Mordell
1052 David Caplan
1053 Maurice Colclough
1054 Tony Bond
1055 Gary Pearce
1056 Richard Cardus
1057 Colin Smart
1058 John Carleton
1059 Les Cusworth
1060 Nick Preston
1061 Phil Blakeway
1062 Clive Woodward
1063 David Cooke
1064 Austin Sheppard
1065 Huw Davies
1066 Nick Jeavons
1067 Bob Hesford
1068 Marcus Rose
1069 Gordon Sargent
1070 John Fidler
1071 Steve Mills
1072 Tony Swift
1073 Peter
       Winterbottom
1074 Nick Stringer
1075 Jim Syddall
1076 Steve Bainbridge
1077 Steve Boyle
1078 David Trick
1079 Nick Youngs
1080 Paul Simpson
1081 Colin White
1082 Jon Hall
1083 Bryan Barley
1084 Rory Underwood
1085 Steve Redfern
1086 Andy Dun
1087 Paul Rendall
1088 Mark Bailey
1089 Chris Butcher
1090 Richard Hill
1091 John Palmer
1092 Malcolm Preedy
1093 Steve Brain
1094 Gary Rees
1095 Stuart Barnes
1096 Gareth Chilcott
1097 Rob Lozowski

1098 Nigel Melville
1099 Nigel Redman
1100 Rob Andrew
1101 Wade Dooley
1102 Richard Harding
1103 John Orwin
1104 Kevin Simms
1105 Simon Smith
1106 Chris Martin
1107 Mike Teague
1108 Mike Harrison
1109 Paul Huntsman
1110 Jamie Salmon
1111 Simon Halliday
1112 Graham Robbins
1113 Fran Clough
1114 Dean Richards
1115 David Cusani
1116 Graham Dawe
1117 Brian Moore
1118 Peter Williams
1119 Jon Webb
1120 Will Carling
1121 Jeff Probyn
1122 Mickey Skinner
1123 Chris Oti
1124 John Bentley
1125 David Egerton
1126 Barry Evans
1127 Andy Robinson
1128 Paul Ackford
1129 Andy Harriman
1130 Dewi Morris
1131 John Buckton
1132 Steve Bates
1133 Jerry Guscott
1134 Simon
       Hodgkinson
1135 Mark Linnett
1136 Andy Mullins
1137 Nigel Heslop
1138 Jason Leonard
1139 David Pears
1140 Dean Ryan
1141 John Olver
1142 Martin Bayfield
1143 Tim Rodber
1144 Ian Hunter

1145 Victor Ubogu
1146 Tony Underwood
1147 Ben Clarke
1148 Phil de Glanville
1149 Martin Johnson
1150 Kyran Bracken
1151 Jon Callard
1152 Neil Back
1153 Steve Ojomoh
1154 Mike Catt
1155 Paul Hull
1156 Graham Rowntree
1157 Richard West
1158 Damian Hopley
1159 John Mallett
1160 Mark Regan
1161 Lawrence Dallaglio
1162 Matt Dawson
1163 Paul Grayson
1164 Jon Sleightholme
1165 Garath Archer
1166 Adedayo Adebayo
1167 Andy Gomarsall
1168 Simon Shaw
1169 Chris Sheasby
1170 Tim Stimpson
1171 Phil Greening
1172 Rob Hardwick
1173 Nick Beal
1174 Richard Hill
1175 Austin Healey
1176 Darren Garforth
1177 Martin Corry
1178 Tony Diprose
1179 Nick Greenstock
1180 Martin Haag
1181 Jim Mallinder
1182 Kevin Yates
1183 Richard Cockerill
1184 Danny Grewcock
1185 Mark Mapletoft
1186 Alex King
1187 Will Green
1188 Will Greenwood
1189 Andy Long
1190 Matt Perry
1191 David Rees
1192 Dorian West

1193 Phil Vickery
1194 Jonny Wilkinson
1195 Scott Benton
1196 Spencer Brown
1197 Richard Pool-Jones
1198 Steve Ravenscroft
1199 Ben Sturnham
1200 Dominic Chapman
1201 Stuart Potter
1202 Josh Lewsey
1203 Pat Sanderson
1204 Tom Beim
1205 Dave Sims
1206 Jos Baxendell
1207 Rob Fidler
1208 Paul Sampson
1209 Dan Luger
1210 Neil McCarthy
1211 Steve Hanley
1212 Barrie-Jon Mather
1213 Trevor Woodman
1214 Joe Worsley
1215 Ben Cohen
1216 Mike Tindall
1217 Iain Balshaw
1218 Julian White
1219 David Flatman
1220 Leon Lloyd
1221 Jason Robinson
1222 Steve Borthwick
1223 Ben Kay
1224 Lewis Moody
1225 Jamie Noon
1226 Michael Stephenson
1227 Dave Walder
1228 Steve White-Cooper
1229 Martyn Wood
1230 Fraser Waters
1231 Olly Barkley
1232 Tom Palmer
1233 Tom Voyce
1234 Charlie Hodgson
1235 Alex Sanderson
1236 Steve Thompson
1237 Nick Duncombe

1238 Henry Paul
1239 Geoff Appleford
1240 Phil Christophers
1241 Alex Codling
1242 Michael Horak
1243 Ben Johnston
1244 James Simpson-Daniel
1245 Robbie Morris
1246 Ollie Smith
1247 Mike Worsley
1248 Stuart Abbott
1249 Dan Scarbrough
1250 Chris Jones
1251 Matt Stevens
1252 Michael Lipman
1253 Andy Titterrell
1254 Tim Payne
1255 Mark Cueto
1256 Andy Hazell
1257 Andrew Sheridan
1258 Hugh Vyvyan
1259 Harry Ellis
1260 Mathew Tait
1261 James Forrester
1262 Duncan Bell
1263 Andy Goode
1264 Mark van Gisbergen
1265 Louis Deacon
1266 Perry Freshwater
1267 Lee Mears
1268 Tom Varndell
1269 Alex Brown
1270 Magnus Lund
1271 Peter Richards
1272 George Chuter
1273 Nick Walshe
1274 Anthony Allen
1275 Shaun Perry
1276 Paul Sackey
1277 Toby Flood
1278 Andy Farrell
1279 Olly Morgan
1280 Tom Rees
1281 Nick Easter
1282 David Strettle
1283 Shane Geraghty

1284 James Haskell
1285 Stuart Turner
1286 Mike Brown
1287 Dean Schofield
1288 Matt Cairns
1289 Darren Crompton
1290 Roy Winters
1291 Ben Skirving
1292 Nick Abendanon
1293 Dan Hipkiss
1294 Luke Narraway
1295 Danny Cipriani
1296 Lesley Vainikolo
1297 Richard Wigglesworth
1298 Tom Croft
1299 Paul Hodgson
1300 Topsy Ojo
1301 Danny Care
1302 David Paice
1303 Jason Hobson
1304 Delon Armitage
1305 Riki Flutey
1306 Nick Kennedy
1307 Ugo Monye
1308 Dylan Hartley
1309 Jordan Crane
1310 Steffon Armitage
1311 Ben Foden
1312 Matt Banahan
1313 Tom May
1314 Dave Wilson
1315 Sam Vesty
1316 Chris Robshaw
1317 Ayoola Erinle
1318 Courtney Lawes
1319 Paul Doran-Jones
1320 Dan Cole
1321 Matt Mullan
1322 Ben Youngs
1323 Chris Ashton
1324 Shontayne Hape
1325 Dave Attwood
1326 Hendre Fourie
1327 Tom Wood
1328 Alex Corbisiero
1329 Manu Tuilagi

1330 Mouritz Botha
1331 Charlie Sharples
1332 Joe Simpson
1333 Brad Barritt
1334 Phil Dowson
1335 Owen Farrell
1336 Geoff Parling
1337 Lee Dickson
1338 Jordan Turner-Hall
1339 Ben Morgan
1340 Rob Webber
1341 Tom Johnson
1342 Joe Marler

1343 Jonathan Joseph
1344 Thomas Waldrom
1345 Alex Goode
1346 Tom Youngs
1347 Mako Vunipola
1348 Joe Launchbury
1349 Freddie Burns
1350 Billy Twelvetrees
1351 Matt Kvesic
1352 Christian Wade
1353 Kyle Eastmond
1354 Billy Vunipola
1355 Henry Thomas

1356 Jonny May
1357 Marland Yarde
1358 Stephen Myler
1359 Joel Tomkins
1360 Jack Nowell
1361 Luther Burrell
1362 George Ford
1363 Joe Gray
1364 Chris Pennell
1365 Semesa
        Rokoduguni
1366 George Kruis
1367 Anthony Watson